How Children Learn at Home

Also available from Continuum

Educating Your Child at Home, Alan Thomas and Jane Lowe

How Children Learn at Home

Alan Thomas and Harriet Pattison

continuum

Continuum International Publishing Group
The Tower Building
11 York Road
London
SE1 7NX

80 Maiden Lane, Suite 704
New York, NY 10038

www.continuumbooks.com

British Library Cataloguing-in-Publication Data
A catalogue record for this book is available from the British Library.

ISBN: 9780826479983 (hardcover)
        9780826479990 (paperback)

Library of Congress Cataloging-in-Publication Data

Thomas, Alan.
  How children learn at home / Alan Thomas and Harriet Pattison.
     p. cm.
  ISBN-13: 978-0-8264-7998-3 (hardcover)
  ISBN-10: 0-8264-7998-7 (hardcover)
  ISBN-13: 978-0-8264-7999-0 (pbk.)
  ISBN-10: 0-8264-7999-5 (pbk.)
  1. Home schooling. I. Pattison, Harriet. II. Title.

LC40.T48 2007
371.04'2--dc22

                    2007020997

Typeset by Free Range Book Design & Production Limited
Printed and bound in Great Britain by Antony Rowe Ltd, Chippenham

Dedication

To Mary and Aled who went to school
and to Tom, Meada and Hope who did not.

Contents

Preface

All children learn at home. From birth onwards they explore the world around them; gradually discovering all sorts of things about their physical and social environment and the culture to which they belong. Casual and undirected though their learning is, infants and young children are able to acquire a prodigious amount of knowledge in the first months and years of life. But we don't expect things to carry on like this for very long. When children start school a dramatic change takes place in the ways that we want them to learn. The informal, 'as and when' learning of life at home is replaced by curricula, timetables, set lessons, teaching aims, testing and monitoring because these are deemed necessary for continued satisfactory learning. There are now however, a growing number of children who either never start school or who opt out at some stage during the next eleven years. Many of these children simply carry on with, or return to, the informal learning that served them so well in infancy. This book is about those children and how they learn.

We came to collaborate on the research we describe in this book by different routes. Alan Thomas, a development psychologist was initially interested in individualized teaching and sought to study it through children educated at home. His first contact was with a home-educating family with whom he 'lived in' for a week. It happened by chance to be a family whose approach was entirely informal. Instead of the individualized teaching he expected to see, nothing of any obvious consequence seemed to happen, at least on the surface. The children, aged nine and thirteen, had their interests, including reading, which occupied for time to time during the week. They all went out a lot because the weather was nice. One of the children went to band practice with his trumpet and the other helped a neighbour with her baby. They talked a lot with their mother and anyone else who came into the house. And that was it. No lessons, no exercises, no teaching. Alan was fascinated and decided to look more closely at informal learning.

Harriet Pattison has a background in social anthropology and the philosophy of science and thus interests in both the nature of knowledge and in how individuals and their culture create one another. Her interest in home education began, as it has done for so many, with her own children. An early unhappy experience of nursery school became the impetus for exploring alternative education and the initial plan for one year at home soon turned into many. Informal home education raises vast numbers of questions but, for Harriet, one stood out above all the others – how on earth do they know *that*? Our book attempts to find some answers to that question.

Pinning down informal learning has often felt very much like trying to catch a sunbeam or shut up a shadow in a box; our understanding has often proved to be as elusive as the subject matter itself. The research we describe in this book has been a journey of exploration and our own adventure in informal learning. Our guides along the way have been the families who took the time to talk to us and share their experiences and thoughts with us. We are very indebted to them for their collaboration in our quest to gain a better understanding of informal learning.

We would also like to thank those who helped us contact home educators whose approach was informal: Susan Wight and the Tasmanian Home Education Advisory Council in Australia; Leonie Baldwin and Andrew Lloyd in Ireland; David Hill, Claire Fairall and Leslie Barson in the UK.

We are grateful to Dr Dorothy Faulkner, Nick Gudge and Professor Judy Ireson for their comments on a working paper which was the basis of Chapter 3.

Finally, sincere thanks to Christina Garbutt of Continuum for both her encouragement and, especially, her toleration.

Chapter 1

Introduction

Over the past twenty years, home education, particularly in Europe, North America, Australia and New Zealand has grown apace and an increasing research interest is now helping to build a larger picture of this trend. So far the focus has rested on such issues as historical development, prevalence, what leads parents to educate their children at home, legal and political issues, and dealings with educational authorities and professionals. While academic outcomes have generally been shown to be favourable (Lines, 2001; Meighan, 1995; Rothermel, 2002), the question of how parents actually go about educating their children at home has received very little attention.

All preschool children learn at home of course. It's what we expect them to do from the moment they are born. By the time they reach school age, regardless of background, children have acquired language (including many abstract concepts), the foundations of literacy and numeracy, a range of practical skills and a considerable amount of general knowledge. By far the greater part of this learning occurs informally during the simple hurly-burly of everyday life. Parents may play a vital role in inducting their children into the culture but it is one of which they are largely unaware. Certainly there is very little, if any, planned and deliberate teaching or application and effort of the kind later expected of children in school. Parents simply expect their children to learn, whilst children themselves are largely unaware that they are learning. Indeed, the achievements of informal learning at this stage of life, although prodigious, are so commonplace that they receive very little recognition in comparison with later *real* learning in school.

After children start school they do, of course, still go on learning informally. They pick up and practise all kinds of knowledge as they go about their lives outside school. Society's reliance on literacy ensures almost constant exposure to the written word both inside and outside the home, managing pocket money, playing board games or becoming familiar with sports statistics may contribute to numeracy. In their free time, children join clubs, pursue hobbies and follow up all sorts of interests at varying levels. But whilst teachers recognize such learning it is generally thought of as peripheral, at best supportive of the specialized structured learning offered in school.

Within the home educating community however, it is widely recognized that this kind of learning can continue well into secondary school age as the main or only form of education. Variously described as 'unschooling' in North America, 'autonomous' or 'child-led' in the UK and 'natural learning' in Australia and New Zealand, personal accounts detailing and supporting this type of learning abound in home education newsletters and magazines and in some longer publications (e.g. Bendell, 1987; Dowty, 2000). The proportion of home-educators relying on informal learning is impossible to gauge. However, in one of very few studies on the subject, Alan Thomas found that, whilst a wide variety of educating styles were to be found among home educators, there was, within this variation, a significant shift towards informal learning (Thomas, 1998). Many parents started out using the familiar structured approach of schools but without the external compulsion to continue in this vein, found themselves drawn towards more informal methods. Children themselves often resisted the 'school at home' approach and besides this, parents found that children were learning spontaneously and effectively outside their planned lessons. The degree to which families gave up formal learning varied. Some felt more comfortable retaining a varying amount of structured input but others abandoned formal learning altogether. This reliance on informal learning clearly represents a radical departure from conventional pedagogy and few from the world of professional education would accept that such an apparently haphazard and hotchpotch way of learning could allow children to satisfactorily develop their intellectual potential.

In this book we seek to gain a better understanding of how informal learning works and how it is able to replace school-based pedagogy. Perhaps both the greatest fascination and the greatest difficulty in studying informal learning is getting to grips with its sheer ordinariness. As will become apparent, informal learning remains, as it is during those first years of life, a commonplace, unremarkable and yet astonishingly efficient way to learn.

Scope of the book

Alan Thomas' previous research described how parents found themselves gravitating away from structured learning and instruction towards informal learning (Thomas, 1998). Why and how this happened became the basis for working towards a greater understanding of children's informal learning. In the next chapter we summarize his earlier work. In Chapter 3 we draw on a range of research that has a bearing on informal learning across the lifespan and which serves as a theoretical backdrop for the study to which the rest of the book is devoted. We also grapple with the problem of pinning down exactly what we mean by informal learning. Chapter 4 onwards deals with our own research, beginning in Chapters 4 and 5 with the 'what' and 'how' of informal learning for children of school age. The former we have called the informal curriculum, which, simply put, is the world around children in their daily lives. How children actually engage with the informal curriculum is the subject of Chapter 5. At a conceptual level we consider three types of learning. Incidental and implicit learning, which both occur with little awareness on the part of the child, and self-directed learning in which children more deliberately find out about something that has captured their interest. The problem, as we show, is that such concepts tell us little about the ways in which children learn on a day-to-day basis. Therefore much of our approach is focused on real-life incidents through which learning can be traced. In Chapter 6 we investigate the part which parents play in their children's learning: as role models, facilitators, co-learners and more experienced members of the culture. Chapter 7 is devoted to play, generally considered to be recreational 'time out' for children in school, but viewed by the parents in our study as an important vehicle for learning. Chapters 8 to 10 are devoted to the informal acquisition of literacy and numeracy.

The participants

The research for this book is predicated on a simple question: How do children of school age learn informally? Of course we had some ideas of our own based on earlier work on home education approaches and other research and theory relevant to informal learning, some of which is discussed in Chapters 2 and 3. Our intention however was to take a 'blue sky' approach in which we asked participants to share their experiences and their own views of informal learning. Our only criterion for interview was that the parents in question described themselves as informal. We did however, work to ensure that a wide range of families took part, from those who had been home educating for a few years with young children to those with much older and adult children who had been educated at home.

Twenty-six parents were interviewed and, in a few instances, their children as well if they so chose. The families ranged between those who had home educated for a couple of years to those with grown-up children who had completed a greater part of their compulsory education informally. Nineteen were obtained by various means: placing an advert in an English regional home education magazine; at meetings of groups of home educators; through home-educating organizations, and one through a chance meeting at a university. Seven were parents who were contacted deliberately because they had been or were active in the home education community and whose experience therefore ranged well beyond their own families. Some of these had contributed to home education magazines and newsletters, appeared in the media and had advised parents who had queries about informal learning. Three families were Australian, three Irish and one Canadian. The rest were British. Each family has been given a number from 1 to 26 and this is cited after every quote taken from that family's interview. Basic family details and corresponding identification numbers are given in the Appendix. One family also contributed more detailed examples of learning in the form of case studies and diary extracts.

Any sample will obviously be restricted to those who are willing to participate and this may mean that less positive or different views of informal learning were not shared with us. Some of the families were members of the same home educating group and may have gravitated together because of shared philosophies and experiences thus perhaps narrowing the range of experiences with which we were coming into contact.

Interviews

As far as the interviews were concerned, very little was prescribed other than telling parents our intention was to find out more about informal learning. In a few instances, children took part, being present throughout or from time to time. It was made clear at the start and end of each interview that participants could withdraw at any time. No one did. Interviews were recorded and transcripts were sent out after the interview. Participants were asked not only to check for accuracy but also invited to erase, edit or add anything they wished, the purpose being to obtain an account that was reflective. All the interviews were carried out by ourselves. Names, where these are used to aid the reading of longer interviews and accounts, have been changed.

It needs to be emphasized that we were seeking to understand what has been described as a very elusive phenomenon – informal learning. We had no agenda and few expectations other than those related to the earlier research or based on what we had read. In our analysis we identify themes but also include individual comments and observations where these seem to further our understanding. One of the fascinations of informal learning is that every family, every child and every educational path is unique. We were not seeking to homogenize experiences or to present any kind of prescriptive blueprint. Rather we simply wanted to make a start in discovering more about an intriguing and fascinating form of learning.

Chapter 2

Towards informal learning

In *Educating Children at Home,* Alan Thomas studied the educational approaches used by 100 home-educating families in the UK and Australia (Thomas, 1998). One of the main findings to emerge from his research was that while most families started out expecting to educate their children in the time-honoured way, by carefully planning lessons based on structured teaching materials, few maintained this over any length of time. Instead, education at home took on a much freer, less pre-ordered and generally informal shape. In this chapter we re-visit this earlier research because it shows how parents are drawn to becoming more and more informal, in some instances abandoning any semblance of structured learning. The increasing dominance of, and reliance on, informal learning sets the scene for the study which forms the bulk of this book.

Even formal learning at home is not like school

For those parents who removed children from school, home education very often began as it is most popularly visualized; an imitation of the classroom with children spending the equivalent of a school day working at desks or the kitchen table and having lessons which their teacher-parents have prepared for them. Parents take on the teaching role by keeping their children on task, asking questions to check their understanding, marking, grading and testing in very much the manner of school. However, even when parents retain the general feeling of 'rightness' about this path of education there is inevitably greater flexibility at home. A timetable is generally found unnecessary and is often dropped altogether. Parents can take advantage of those times when their children are most receptive, including the evenings and weekends. On the other hand, if a child is obviously not learning effectively for whatever reason then lessons can be put off until another time.

At home, lessons tend to be concentrated and intensive. This is mainly due to extra individual attention and also because very little time is spent on the kind of peripheral activities such as administration and classroom management which take up much of classroom time. In consequence, not only lessons but the entire working day is shortened, generally restricted to part of the morning.

By far the most important difference between more formal, structured learning at home and in school though, is that learning at home becomes an individualized and interactive process. Parents repeatedly refer to being able to strike while the iron is hot, to deal with problems as they arise and to avoid going on to something new until the prerequisite knowledge or concepts have been acquired. There is little shared learning in school, if only because most of what is taught is carefully prepared by the teacher beforehand. In fact, being on top of the material to be taught is a hallmark of good classroom practice, but shared learning is an everyday feature of home education, especially as children grow older and move into areas their parents know little about or have forgotten from their own schooling. This would not do in the classroom, but at home it probably enhances the quality of learning because the children are active partners in the process rather than passive recipients of adult-administered knowledge. Sometimes children jump ahead of their parents in a new area, leading them to gain in confidence in their own learning as well as seeing that it is quite acceptable for an adult not to know. The extent to which shared learning is a reality is revealed by the number of parents who say that educating their child has extended their own knowledge and in some cases helped them to get a full grasp of concepts only half understood from their own schooling. In the following extract a mother and child aged eleven have been working together on algebraic fractions. It's an extremely shortened account of what happened over the course of at least an hour. They are both struggling to understand but there's no feeling of failure. There's a sense of knowing they will eventually work through it successfully.

> *Mother*: Oh Jesus! ...
> [she is having difficulty with addition of algebraic fractions; she eventually seems to manage and asks her son to explain it to her using numerical fractions. He writes 1/2 + 1/3 and works out with her how the algebraic answer is arrived at. She goes off to the next room to work with her other child. He writes the algebraic solution. She returns to check, gives praise and goes to the other room again. He goes on to subtraction of algebraic fractions, then calls his mother for help and she comes back into the room.]
> *Mother*: It's the same system.
> *Child*: No it isn't.
> *Mother*: Yes it is ...
> [She demonstrates and he seems to follow. They move on to multiplication. His mother has a go without success but inspires him to try again. She goes

off again and he seems to work it out. No he doesn't. He goes to fetch her.]
Mother: Multiply top by top and bottom by bottom.
Child: Does it always work?
Mother: I don't know.
Child: Shall I try something to see?
Mother: Yes, multiply the denominators together – the bottoms.
Child: What do you mean, multiply them together?
[They continue and check the answer arithmetically. Both still seem unsure.]
Mother: [to me] I think he's had enough anyway. [She goes out of the room.]
[He continues to work at multiplication and seems to understand. He goes in search of his mother who is now in the toilet.]
Child: [shouting and banging on the toilet door] I know how to do it! (Thomas, 1998: 49).

Moving towards informal learning

A more fundamental pedagogical change occurs as parents gradually discover the potential of informal teaching and learning. There is nothing in the way children learn in school to suggest how powerful informal learning might be. Two influences impel parents towards informal styles of learning. The first is the result of their own observations, the second the reaction of their children to structured and direct teaching.

Although parents may continue to ensure that academic material is covered in a manner they believe most schools would approve of, with experience they become aware of other ways of learning rarely encountered in school. Most common was a growing awareness of how much learning took place through spontaneous conversation, both incidentally and sometimes at great depth (see also Thomas, 1994). In addition they noticed that their children seemed to learn a great deal by following their own interests.

> At first I was very strict and regimented with a timetable in the morning. I got all the necessary books but I later realised I was stifling the children. I've loosened up now. We've learnt that home education is not school at home. I've had to throw out so many schoolish approaches. They start with half an hour piano and then do some maths and English in the morning. The rest of the day is free. But I'm mingling with them all the time – following them up with whatever they are doing. (p. 55)

Parents who find the informal approach appealing often feel that they are moving into uncertain territory. They want to strike a reasonable balance but may be unsure where to draw the line.

> We floundered a bit in the early years, not knowing what direction to go in and trying to get a balance between regimented and relaxed. (p. 56)

> They have schoolwork in the morning from 10 am ... All this is more for my benefit than theirs. I need to know the basic things are being covered. I think they'd cover it anyway ... (p. 57)

There is clearly a dilemma for 'middle-of-the-road' parents who recognize the contribution of informal learning but who also fear that it offers no guarantee that children will acquire essential basic knowledge and skills. It can be very hard, on a day-to-day basis at least, to show that informal learning is working. At school, daily evidence of learning, usually in the form of written work, is an integral part of the system. Teachers in school regularly assess their pupils and are expected to know with some precision what they have taught and what pupils have learned. It takes courage to question let alone depart from the security of this highly professionalized system. Yet parents' own observations frequently pushed them towards doing precisely that.

Children's resistance to formal teaching and learning

Most parents might not have departed greatly from the security of structured learning if they had not also been influenced by their children. Because children are at home with someone familiar they are much more able to influence the way in which they learn.

One of the most powerful ways children at home have of making their parents question structured teaching and learning is by 'turning off' if they do not understand or by simply losing interest. In the classroom, children are at least expected to give outward signs of attention or concentration, though this does not mean they are actually gaining any benefit from what they are listening to or doing. Feigning attention to the teacher and concentration on tasks set by the teacher have almost become art forms. In the classroom, children are not excused from a lesson if they are not listening or are failing to produce work in the desired manner. We accept this and tacitly acknowledge there is not much the teacher can do other than encourage, exhort, threaten a punishment or promise a reward, activities which take up much of a teacher's time. But it is different at home. Parents are acutely aware when their children stop listening or are not engaged in any work they are doing and are able to abandon their own efforts accordingly. There is simply no point in continuing when children are not listening, or going on asking for more effort if they are not responding.

At home, unlike school, you can simply stop, do something else, even take the day off if you like. This makes sense if only because there can be nothing as unproductive as insisting on teaching someone who is not learning. However, some families found that their children consistently resisted anything that smacked of 'lesson'.

> I had positive ideas about some kind of instruction. I wasn't going to leave him to play all day. For a while we had a time when he did work every morning for a while ... Then there was a big reaction against this, definitely. Then we stopped doing anything formal in an obvious way for nine months or a year. It used to lead to arguments and a charged atmosphere ... You worry that communication has broken down. (p. 59)

It is not that home-educated children cannot adapt to the kind of teaching and learning found in school. Most do, if they eventually go, or return, to school. But many do resist it at home. One parent, a teacher, recognized that optimal classroom and home pedagogies might be qualitatively different.

> [At home] we offer, but do not demand. [In school] I support more formal schooling and the national curriculum because that's what works best in school. (p. 59)

When children in school resist learning the obvious assumption is that, for whatever reason, they do not want to learn. This may be unfair because there are few productive opportunities in school for doing other than the teacher bids. At home, on the other hand, children seem to spend most of their time in some useful activity aside from or instead of structured learning.

> There's a bit of maths, English and spelling most mornings, but it always means I have to interrupt what she's doing, and she's always been able to occupy herself productively. (p. 60)

The following quote on the home-educating experiences of a mother and son, shows how both these factors, resistance and parental reflection, played a role in shaping their eventual views on informal learning. The fourteen-year-old-boy was taken out of school when he was eleven, as a last resort. The main reason was that he was being bullied. But he had also been a thorn in the side of his teachers from the earliest years because they could not get him to do more than a minimal amount of work. Both they and his mother were equally perplexed. He was apparently making normal progress with a minimum of effort. After his mother took him out his attitude to formal learning did not change one whit. He just didn't like being taught. When he came out of school his mother attempted to emulate school practice at home, the only way forward that she knew. She thought he was not cooperating with his work in school because he was ill at ease. Now that he was removed, she expected him to get down to work. But he behaved towards her just as he had to his teachers.

Work did eventually get done on sufferance, with no end of rows and tears and exasperation on both our parts and a total lack of comprehension on my part. Why wouldn't he do anything? He was always alert and asking questions. But he wouldn't do formal academic work. For two or three years it was hell. I was constantly threatening school: 'If you are just going to gaze out of the window you might just as well do that in school' ... I got as far as ringing the school for an appointment to go back, but I knew that was just for my benefit. When it came to it I knew I was instinctively doing the right thing by keeping him out. But I'd given up work and he didn't meet us half way. That was very hard to accept.

I borrowed school books to see what children his age were doing. I made sure I understood everything before getting him to do it. Then I'd get fed up with the battle and say 'Go your own way' and he would for two weeks and then I'd get guilty again, feeling I was letting him down if I let him get away with doing too little work. It was so difficult when he wouldn't do anything. After battling all day I didn't want him as a son.

He would sit and read fiction and non-fiction and do jigsaws for hours. He'd spend hours and hours working on his bike and riding it. He'd do gardening. He'd clean the house from top to bottom after I'd just asked him to do his own room. He's never been afraid of work.

I couldn't keep up the pressure. It was too much for me. I asked him what he least wanted to do and we cut that out. We agreed we'd just do English, maths and science for GCSE and let the rest go – the other 5 or so subjects. I said 'I want you to be numerate, literate and have a knowledge of the world around.' We started ploughing through Letts books. He was doing it more willingly. I could trust him to go to his room and he'd do it painfully slowly. He needn't have been slow. He was capable of working much faster. I've found the Letts National Curriculum pleasantly set out and most useful. Going through the books gave me confidence, but I was finding a lot of the work crushingly boring too, so how could I argue that he shouldn't?

But the more I did the more I asked: What's the point of this? Why write things down just to have them on a piece of paper? It's said you do this to revise, but it was pointless. If he'd been more malleable he'd have been forced. It was his strength that did it. I got every book on education I could ...

I now feel that what I did to try and force him was wrong. Now I'd say – leave the child alone for a year. Don't try and cultivate interests. I booked a tour round Westminster Abbey. The tour guide asked him: 'Are you interested in history?' 'No' he answered: 'My Mum is ...'

At present there's no academic work. He read Lord of the Flies and Animal Farm at 12. We discussed them afterwards. He gave me perfectly good answers, but if I said: 'Write it down' – nothing.

I gave him a comprehension test ... He asked: 'What for? I don't need to know about the leaning tower of Pisa.' I said what the idea of comprehension was. He said: 'You know I can do that.' I said that was what they expect in an exam, but that's not a good reason for doing it. It's me who's imposed the pressure. I found it very hard to accept that what we do now is the best way. It's taken me four years to get here. (p. 62–4 abridged)

A natural way forward?

Most of what children learn during the early years, including the foundations for literacy and numeracy on which much of the primary curriculum is based, is acquired informally, largely through everyday interaction with their parents/carers. There is no developmental or educational logic behind the radical change in pedagogy from informal to formal when children start school and there is no reason, *a priori*, why this cultural apprenticeship of early childhood cannot be extended through the primary school years and beyond. For some it simply felt the natural way forward.

These parents, recognizing their children had been progressing intellectually throughout the first few years of life, simply continued and extended on what they were already doing.

> We felt there was nothing to lose. Why interrupt something that had been going on from before the age of five? (p. 32)

> School seems unnatural. With a huge effort and cost and sometimes pain, you try to get something into the children which would happen anyway. (p. 128)

Although their routes to the same conclusion varied, many parents came to recognize the potential of informal learning and to trust it, sometimes hedging their bets by retaining a certain amount of structured learning, usually confined to an hour or two a day but not on all days by any means. Family events such as visiting grandparents or the birth of a new relative, an outing or simply a fine day can take preference. Others abandoned structure altogether although often with a lingering acknowledgement of the formal route.

> Sometimes I think we should do something but mostly things just happen … she often goes to a friend's house and sometimes they just play all day, role play and games and make things, puppets and dolls and bead threading. I started off more formally doing work but gave it up because [she] began to find it boring … I still think they should do something but mostly things just happen. (p. 57)

> We're trying to maintain a routine of one hour on Monday and one hour on Tuesday, but we are lucky if we can manage that. (p. 58)

For these families learning and daily living became inextricably intertwined, making it very hard to identify what is happening in an educational sense.

> At first she said we should go in and show her work [to the school headteacher], and we did, but this quickly lapsed. I felt somehow it was for me to put on a performance for her ... I used to set things up for them and go to great lengths to explain to them, but not anymore ... I now see us as carrying on living rather than me 'educating' them. (p. 58)

And this response from one parent would scandalize most teachers as well as parents of children in school.

> Sometimes days go by without anything special happening. (p. 68)

Trying to capture informal learning

Informal learning is not restricted to childhood. Throughout life we are constantly picking up knowledge casually and incidentally in the context of everyday activities, at work, socially and at home, often with little awareness that we are actually learning anything. We may also learn a great deal by deliberately following an interest or hobby. Informal home education allows a glimpse of just how powerful both these kinds of learning can be.

In casual or incidental learning concepts are acquired, skills improved and new knowledge gained during the course of concrete, everyday activities. An activity, from the child's point of view, may be helping to make cakes, going for a walk, shopping, going out in the car, reading a book, making a house out of a cardboard box, and so on. Any learning episodes, in maths, language, science, geography or whatever, are not differentiated but are simply part and parcel of the concrete activity. They may be integral to the activity, such as maths in shopping and science in cooking, or incidental to it, occurring through social conversation, during a walk, in the car or at mealtimes. From the child's point of view it is the activity which is paramount although what might be considered more intellectual elements of learning may also be advanced. Learning is therefore embedded and contextualized in a way it rarely can be in formal lessons.

Partly because of this, increments in this kind of learning are extremely difficult to pin down. Fortuitously, one parent provided a very detailed record of her child's learning over a number of years. Maths was chosen to illustrate progress in informal learning because it was most easily differentiated in the diaries. It was therefore possible to tease out the way in which the child's mathematical competence increased between the ages of 7 and 11. Put together, informal activities and experiences at home covered much the same ground as the primary school maths curriculum. However, the child in question did not really 'do' maths, certainly not in the formal sense. She helped with cooking and shopping, went on car journeys, collected supermarket 'trolley money' and came to appreciate the value of material goods, all of which included maths, but she did not see it like that. She saw only the concrete activity. If she did sometimes count money or do 'sums' in her head, as she acknowledged on one occasion, it was her decision, sparked by her emerging understanding or simple curiosity about number. The point is that maths, certainly most of what is acquired at the primary level, can be learned as an integral part of everyday concrete activities. In school, maths has to be divorced from the dynamic realities of everyday life.

This leads to another problem in tracing the course of informal learning; it is not ordered or sequential in the sense that it is in school, though the sequence obviously makes sense to the child. A curriculum or a programme of learning would be deemed very poor indeed if it were not logically developed and graded into digestible morsels. However, in the maths example just mentioned, progress was by no means linear. There were apparently inexplicable advances and regressions, things were learned and then forgotten or suddenly grasped without what would appear to be basic prerequisite knowledge. This is in contrast to the smooth upward progression expected in school and could lead to parental frustration with the apparent muddle of informal learning.

> Last night I was feeling that [my daughter's] home ed. is leading nowhere ,,, I feel like we just seem to have a whole heap of false starts which we fail to follow up, a bag of bits and pieces which aren't forming anything concrete. (p. 81)

Yet somehow or other the children seem to emerge with an education that enables them to enter the world of work or further their education by formal means.

Parents themselves could often only attest to, rather than explain, informal learning. They were often unaware of specifically what their children were learning and it was only when they looked back over what they had done, or kept a careful record that they could see how much learning had taken place. One mother visualized her daughter's learning as a weaving process that drew information and ideas together and it was only when she looked back that what she called 'threads' appeared and patterns emerged, as this parent also pointed out.

> A lot of what happens might appear to a school teacher to be fleeting, inconsequential and muddled – but part of this is the opportunity there is to drop and pick up interests as and when you want. (p. 70)

Not all learning, however, is this casual; even very young children pursue understanding with purpose and deliberation and indeed we expect children to acquire a great deal of general knowledge beyond what might be simply picked up. At home such learning is still informal in that it is not planned beforehand, but projects and topics can be pursued for days, weeks or longer. Children can follow through on anything that captures their interest, either under their own steam or with the more active support of their parent. One of the consequences of this is that learning is an enjoyable experience – informal learners are doing what they want to do and are therefore motivated learners.

> What I taught her was research skills. That's all you need to find out about any subject. We'd go to the library and just pick out books she was interested in. Once she asked me about government. We went into the whole Westminster system, back to Cromwell. (p. 75)

> Topics tend to crop up because they are sparked off by something, for example, they went to an event in which they dressed up as Tudor peasants and this led to a project on the Stuarts which lasted for months. (p. 75)

So, how far have we got?

Informal learning for all children during the first years of life, and for these children after reaching school age, might be described in terms of an open-ended cultural apprenticeship. By sharing in the life of the family children are quite naturally exposed to the workings of their culture and to the skills and intellectual understanding which are necessary for operating within it. In a sense, the family and wider culture provide an 'informal curriculum' in which, unlike school, intellectual content is largely undifferentiated. We deal with this informal curriculum in Chapter 4.

The next question is how does this cultural apprenticeship work out in practice? Children need ways to engage with and to make sense of their environment and they need to be able to cast new experiences in the light of the things that they already know. In other words they need to be able to impose their own sequence on to the informal curriculum. One of the strengths of informal learning may in fact be that children are able to do this and are not faced with having to try to digest new knowledge which does not fit into or extend what they already know or does not arouse their curiosity or motivation. With informal learning, it is the learner who must decide, consciously or unconsciously, when to concentrate, to attempt something difficult or to repetitively go over something in order to consolidate it. The logic of curriculum sequence may make sense to adults but it does not necessarily equate to a child's developing knowledge base. The latter is determined by the complex and dynamic interaction between the child's level of knowledge, interest, motivation etcetera, as well as the possibilities of direct or indirect contributions from other people and the environment. The processes through which these are put into effect are explored in Chapter 5.

Chapter 3

Other perspectives on informal learning

In this chapter we broaden our perspective on informal learning by reviewing some of the research which has been carried out across the lifespan. We begin with learning in infancy and early childhood, almost by definition informal. For children of school age there is very little research to go on – nearly all children are in school – but there is some illuminating cross-cultural research. Finally, we look at adult informal learning, mostly undertaken in work situations. In different ways, these various research initiatives, together with the work described in the previous chapter, serve as a backdrop for the study presented in the rest of this book.

Early learning

Traditionally, child development research has concentrated on three areas of intellectual growth. The first area, information processing, is concerned with basic cognitive processes such as memory and attention. The second takes a Piagetian approach, charting stages in the development of logical thought. Interesting though these are in their own rights, neither approach takes account of how children experience everyday life nor what they learn on a day-to-day basis. Both perspectives tend to give 'the impression that mental activity springs, fully formed, out of a developmental vacuum' (Wood, 1998: 93).

The third approach comes nearer to explaining early (and later) learning as it focuses on everyday social situations. There are two distinct theoretical strands underlying this approach. The first is based on an expectation that children will simply acquire cultural knowledge. Super and Harkness (1982, 1986) encapsulate this process through their concept of the developmental niche, referring to the physical and social setting in which a newborn baby's life begins. In this niche, day-to-day existence and routine is structured for the infant through such matters as sleep expectations, number and variety of caregivers and other lifestyle features. These in turn are decided by both parental beliefs and values and individual and cultural circumstances. Adapting to the niche is therefore also the beginning of adapting to wider society. Cole (1998), drawing on the work of Super and Harkness, uses the idea of the developmental niche to contrast the sleeping patterns of Kenyan and American infants. Their parents live very different lifestyles in very different circumstances and this quickly becomes reflected in the sleeping patterns of their babies.

Super and Harkness (1998) make it clear that parents behave as they do because of the way their culture operates rather than in order to deliberately teach their infants certain behaviour patterns. However, while their work may help to explain socio-cultural development, they do not address learning of a cognitive nature though this must also be taking place within the developmental niche. The assumption seems to be that this is a different type of learning which, presumably, requires deliberate instruction. This leads us to the second theoretical strand found within the socio-cultural approach. In this, thinking has been overwhelmingly based on the work of the Russian psychologist, Lev Vygotsky. The basic idea is that adults set tasks or activities, ascertain the child's level of knowledge and from there provide step-by-step support which allows the child to complete, with adult help, an activity they could not do by themselves. The term 'zone of proximal development' refers to the difference between what the child is able to achieve alone and what they can accomplish with assistance. It is when progressing within this zone that learning is deemed to be taking place. The adult support which allows a child to operate in the zone of proximal development is often termed as 'scaffolding' referring to the way in which it can be gradually withdrawn as the child's competence increases.

A good deal of research has taken place within this framework, investigating the ways in which parents or carers provide scaffolding and considering the most efficient ways in which this can be offered. David Wood, very much in this tradition, describes how mothers use contingent instructional techniques when helping their children in a pre-planned task (Wood, Wood & Middleton, 1978). Rogoff (1990) portrays transmission of knowledge through what she calls 'guided participation' provided by the parent or other adults. Gauvain (2001) describes the 'active and varied efforts that parents and others make to support, organise and direct children's intellectual growth … arranging for specific learning activities to occur' (p. 11) and 'breaking learning down into manageable segments and then directing the child's attention and efforts to manageable sub-goals' (p. 56).

While there is little doubt that Vygotskian theory has a part to play in explaining how young children learn from more knowledgeable adults, it can hardly explain learning across the board. On a practical level it does not make allowance for everyday reality. Parents tend to bring up their children in busy situations in which they may have to juggle a number of demands; concentrating on the child's development, even if this is seen as desirable, is something that has to be fitted in. Children have simply got to learn a great deal for themselves, a task they undertake vigorously from birth as they explore the environment around them. They begin to anticipate the everyday routine, to initiate interaction with others and to acquire a sense of how they themselves can alter the events and objects surrounding them. Research with babies and infants emphasizes these pro-active exploratory efforts (e.g. Bremner, 1994; Schaffer, 1996).

The proactive aspect of learning has led others to challenge the Vygotskian stress on parental guidance, assistance and scaffolding, based on the 'classical assumption ... that children learn because they are taught' (Trevarthen, 1995: 97). Hoogsteder, M., Maier, R. and Elbers, E. (1998) for example, while acknowledging that research into parental scaffolding of children's learning has been highly influential, argue that it has its limitations. As they explain:

> ... researchers of adult-child interaction tend to connect the child's learning in an interaction rigidly to the instructive behaviour of the adult. The origin of this view is, we think, their educational interest in how educators can most effectively stimulate a child's development. Research was designed in order to explore which kind of instruction is most useful for children ... However, there is more to children's learning than following the adult lead ... a child's persistence in following his or her own way is not necessarily unconstructive .... the child's learning does not necessarily depend on the adult's correct and proper way of intervening (p. 179–80).

Trevarthen (1995) argues that more attention needs to be paid to the extent and nature of children's input in terms of their own self-motivated, creative, pro-active exploration of their world. This type of pro-activity is graphically illustrated by Tizard and Hughes (1984) who recorded talk between young children and their mothers. These conversations reveal the children's purposeful inquiry into the nature of the physical and social world surrounding them. They ask questions and pursue subjects, intent on building up their own understanding in ways which have been described by the authors as 'intellectual search'. Through self-initiated inquiries, children develop their own logical trains of thought, using their parents as a resource to fill some of the self-identified gaps in their own knowledge and, in a very real sense, doing their own scaffolding. Here is one of a myriad of examples from their research on how young children relate to and construct their understanding of the world around them.

> Vida, possibly confused by a well known children's tv programme, thought that clocks told the days of the week. She was playing with a toy clock, and the day was Wednesday:
> *Child*: Where's Wednesday?
> *Mother*: Where's Wednesday?
> *Child*: Mm.
> *Mother*: Today.
> *Child*: Where is it? Which number?

Mother: It's here.
Child: Where?
Mother: Where? Oh, no, you don't have it on the clock, you have it on a calendar.
Child: Oh.
(Tizard & Hughes, 1984: 129)

In the first year of school, children are able, to some extent, to maintain their proactive approach to learning, even if it conflicts with teacher expectations. Ireson and Blay (1999) in their research into adult–child interaction in a naturally occurring activity in a nursery school focused on the role of adult guidance in number development in line with Rogoff's notion of 'guided participation' and related constructs. However, they found this framework to be inadequate because it did not encompass the kind of things which children were doing for and by themselves, in this case building with lego. In fact they found that taking the child's perspective led them to reinterpret adult involvement. As they conclude:

> What from the adult's point of view may be leading the child forward in terms of number development may, from the child's point of view, be a distraction from the explicit task of building … the child is not only an active learner, but an active partner in constructing the activity itself. (p. 35).

Language acquisition is an area of early learning in which children pick up a great deal for themselves. Although there are a number of competing theories, they all have had to deal with the fact that language is acquired informally and involves very little that could be readily identified as direct teaching. While adult–child interaction may be crucial to the process, this takes place amidst the chaotic milieu of everyday existence with little awareness of either teaching or learning. The proactive role of the child is even more evident in other cultures where children are expected to learn without the kind of interaction thought to be essential in Western society (Schieffelin & Ochs, 1998). Whatever the case, there is little doubt that it is the children themselves who have to learn how their language is structured and the many ways in which it holds meaning. Further evidence of this is provided by the way in which young children can acquire a second language with apparent ease when they are immersed in it, as would be the case in the nursery or kindergarten class in school. Where the opportunity is given, language learning can also proceed apace in the same manner in older children or adults. One such case which many expatriate or dual language families might relate to is described by Long (1998) whose eight-year-old daughter became fluent in Icelandic, well ahead of her parents' more formal efforts to learn the language, simply through social interaction with new-found friends following the family's move to that country. Informal to the point of chaotic with input and structure left to chance, yet language learning of this kind is undeniably efficient and an unremarkable commonplace where the opportunities exist.

There is, however, very little in the way of theory outside the instructional framework to suggest how children may learn from adults without direct teaching. Clearly language is an important exception but the possibilities may extend much further. Wherever children grow up they are going to be exposed to the activities of others as they conduct their normal everyday lives. This point is picked up by Schaffer (1996: 239) who proposes that even numeracy may be extended simply by overhearing adult conversations and being party to adult activities.

> The growth of numeracy skills. ... Has for the most part been treated as a purely interpersonal development [but this ...] neglects the fact that from the beginning children are exposed to adult conversations that are full of references to number, made quite spontaneously and with no particular intention to teach ... Thus children's developing cognitive competencies to deal with number are given every opportunity in the course of daily life to become interwoven with the way in which society makes use of numeracy.

That children might learn from such exposure obviously presupposes the active role of the child as learner who must somehow make sense of what is heard by consciously or unconsciously linking it to other information, or possibly without deliberate intent, squirrelling it away to be drawn on later.

Learning through play

Play is a universal feature of childhood although it is only during the last hundred years or so that it has been associated with learning. In play, children's pro-activity is plain to see as they create, direct and maintain their own activities.

> Within minutes of being presented with 'props' [children] are creating detailed and sustained play activities. In these activities they recreate the world they experience outside and inside school. They cook, clean and polish; they plan, travel and explore; they fall ill, are hospitalized and recover; they teach, scold and punish; they fall in love, get married and have children ... There is hardly any area of life that cannot be found in children's play. (Hall, 1994: 114)

Most developmental research has concentrated on cognitive stages of play (sensorimotor, symbolic, rule-governed games) and on socio-emotional factors that enhance or impede participation in social play. Little is actually known about play as a vehicle for learning though many early-childhood educators, influenced by the work of Montessori, Froebel, Isaacs and others, have assumed its relevancy. In fact, the early childhood classroom is the one area of schooling in which there is a heavy reliance on informal learning through play. For example, in the 'home corner' there are opportunities for extending mathematical knowledge through measuring quantities, setting out tables, sharing, etc.; in water and sand play children are assumed to learn about volume and weight; socio-dramatic play involves aspects of literacy such as narrative, vocabulary building and expression. It has also been variously suggested that play offers ways to practise mature skills, to consolidate learning and experience, explore new situations, experiment and create within a secure framework, develop flexibility, problem-solving skills and understanding.

Broadly speaking, there are two competing ideologies concerning play as a vehicle for learning in the early years, one in favour of adult direction and the other of 'free flow' child-directed play. In teacher-directed play, teachers are expected to take advantage of any opportunities to extend learning during play sessions. Hence, it is deemed good practice to interact with children in order to extend vocabulary, make comparisons, ask questions, develop numeracy and so on. In fact there is a fear that children will not learn anything useful without careful preparation of play material and teacher intervention. For example, inspectors from the Office for Standards in Education reported that many teachers failed to exploit the potential of play and cautioned that it should be planned with educational management in mind (OFSTED, 1993). Similarly, the Qualifications and Curriculum Authority maintain that children will only learn through play with effective adult support (QCA, 2000). On the other hand, Bruce (1994, 2004) is a leading proponent of 'free-flow play' with its greater emphasis on intrinsic motivation, choice, control, active use of first-hand experience and a high level of imaginative, creative, innovative and original functioning, arguing that this is sufficient for learning to take place without adult direction other than provision of play materials.

Yet how much play contributes to learning is impossible to say. In spite of all that has been written on the topic, any attempt to assess the significance of play to learning, whether in or out of the classroom, is beset by difficulties. To start with, play encompasses a very wide range of activities from what appears to be nothing more than desultory or meaningless repetition, to highly challenging and intellectual ones. But even judging at this level of observation is fraught; as Ireson and Blay (1999) point out above, what adults might see in the activity is not necessarily what children derive from it.

Furthermore it is next to impossible to separate out learning which has occurred through play from learning that has arisen through other activities (Smith, 1994). Perhaps this is why there is no hard evidence regarding play's contribution to learning, certainly not in school. In fact, Bennett, Wood and Rogers (1996) have criticized what they describe as the prescriptive nature of both ideologies underpinning play as little more than mantras based on untested assumptions.

Children of school age

The kind of informal learning at home we describe in this book would simply not be feasible, or even make sense, in a class of 25 children, although there have been attempts to introduce less formal learning into school. However, the term 'informal learning' has been used in relation to school, usually pejoratively because there is a popular and negative perception that the term implies the kind of excessively permissive education that was supposed to have been in vogue during the 1960s and 1970s. In reality it was very much associated with child-centred learning in which there had been a growing interest during the first half of the twentieth century (e.g. Entwistle, 1970). What this term meant varied tremendously but the general intention was to individualize teaching in the classroom and give children a certain amount of choice in their learning, thus loosening some of the usual restraints of formal learning (Blyth, 1988; Thomas, 1992). The high point for this less formal (not informal) approach to learning came with the publication of the Plowden Report (1967). However, both individualization and choice hardly ventured beyond the rhetorical whilst traditional forms of direct teaching, practice and drill remained unchanged, as two subsequent major classroom studies clearly demonstrated (Bennett, Desforges, Cockburn & Wilkinson, 1984; Galton, Simon & Croll, 1980). Recently, however, the potential role of teaching assistants in relation to informal learning has received some attention (Thomas, 2005).

We are also not concerned with the North American use of the term informal learning to describe hands-on activities in school and outside visits, all arising from set teaching objectives.

Once children reach school age, learning is assumed to require a formal structure and consequently there is very little research into informal learning, certainly not with regard to how it might replace formal schooling. Yet there is no reason to suppose that children stop learning informally even if opportunities for doing so are markedly curtailed. Opie and Opie (1959) describe flourishing and enduring children's cultures handed on entirely informally both within and outside school. Paradise (1998) cites the success of out-of-school learning in such spheres of popular culture as music, language genres, dress, cars and sports. Guberman (1999) points to the part played by number in children's rhymes and games, sometimes involving imaginative adaptations of what might be taught in school, and how these lead to the acquisition of mathematical skills with little or no formal instruction. Medrich, Roizen, Rubin and Buckley (1982) based on a comprehensive survey of children's lives outside school, also show how informal learning contributes to intellectual as well as social development. More striking however, is informal learning which very obviously covers the same subject matter as school, only more efficiently, as in the pioneering study of informal street learning (Carraher, Carraher & Schliemann, 1985). They describe how, as customers, they bought fruit and vegetables from children working part time on a market stall. The children calculated prices of multiple purchases without error, though when the same calculations were subsequently set as classroom tasks they made lots of mistakes. This kind of finding has been confirmed in numerous studies (e.g. Saxe, 1991).

Guberman (1999) similarly describes independent learning in which there is no intention to teach but an expectation that children will somehow learn for themselves. In her research, in Brazil, she studied parents who routinely sent their children on errands, setting the task differently according to the child's capabilities. A young child will first be given the correct money, later there will be instructions for the child to collect the change, then to check the change and later still to calculate the whole transaction for themselves. From the outside this may appear to be a supported progression or scaffolding but from the parent's viewpoint, quite the opposite was happening with the parent acting to extract reliable, helpful assistance from children with the emphasis on ensuring that the child did not overstep their capabilities and mishandle the transaction. Parents may act deliberately to restrict rather than encourage their children's progression in order to make sure that the shopping goes smoothly. They rely on the child to increase knowledge independently and then increase the responsibility attached to the task.

How learning in school and informal learning out of school cross over, influence and affect each other is far from clear though home background, especially parenting, has been associated with educational achievement since the pioneering research of Douglas (1967). Desforges and Abouchaar (2003) reviewing the literature on how parental involvement effects schooling outcomes refer to the many forms which such involvement can take including 'the provision of a secure and stable environment, intellectual stimulation, parent-child discussion, good models of constructive social and educational values and high aspirations relating to personal fulfilment and good citizenship' (p. 4). This type of involvement, they conclude, is critical to success or failure in school, outweighing all other factors in school achievement. Their list does not refer to planned and deliberate pedagogical input or teaching by parents, but does suggest that informal learning is taking place on an intellectual plane, through discussion for instance, as well as promoting positive educational values and attitudes.

Outside school, children may be able to experiment with, practise and adapt what is transmitted in school, allowing them to make sense of what they have learned on their own terms. As long ago as the early part of the last century, Smith (1924, cited in Guberman, 1999) investigated the uses of arithmetic in the out-of-school life of First Grade children. The main activities were children's shop transactions, games involving number, reading Roman numerals on clocks and Arabic ones when finding pages in books, using fractions to divide food with friends, using toy money banks and playing shop. Guberman also provides more recent examples of children learning to understand, and thereby gain control of counting out games and of finding mathematical solutions to problems posed by board games such as Monopoly. These informal activities, or others such as reading for enjoyment, may not just reinforce learning that has already taken place in school but also extend to new learning.

The experience of some students at Summerhill School in Suffolk also points to informal learning of school material. The school has regular timetabled lessons though attendance has not been compulsory since it opened in 1921 in keeping with its philosophy that students should have full responsibility for their own education. Some students do not attend lessons in certain subjects for considerable periods, as much as two years or so, most commonly in the years immediately prior to starting courses at 14 which lead to public examinations. Yet even in a subject as highly structured as maths, it seems that pupils who have missed out a great deal are able to catch up in a very short time. The most likely explanation is that these children have, somehow or other, progressed informally. This was acknowledged, if reluctantly, during an appeal hearing of the Independent Schools Tribunal at the Royal Courts of Justice, after government OFSTED inspectors demanded that lessons be made compulsory, an order which would effectively have closed the school. Empirical support for this kind of learning outside lessons can be found in a study of children's intellectual progress during the long US summer vacation which continued at the same rate as it had done in school, though not for children from a disadvantaged background (Heyns, 1978).

Adults

Most research with adults deals with informal learning in the workplace. Lave and Wenger (1991) for example studied informal apprenticeships, describing how novice butchers, midwives, quartermasters and tailors gradually become competent practitioners through 'situated learning'. The idea is that the learner gains experience in a 'community of practice' in which some members are fully fledged participants and others are not. To begin with the novice is quite marginal but through a collaborative process in which the learner participates to an increasing degree and with increasing responsibility, expertise is gradually acquired. Lave and Wenger term this process 'legitimate peripheral participation' and see it as being primarily a social situation in which the learner acquires the behavioural 'culture' of a group. Gradually they acquire the necessary skills and knowledge to operate effectively and be accepted as a fully fledged member, an adult version of the 'development niche' described earlier. Carraher and Schliemann (2000) show that even mathematical knowledge can be acquired in this way. They describe how experienced carpenters, with little schooling, informally acquired a better understanding of aspects of maths relevant to their work than carpenter apprentices enrolled in classes specifically aimed at teaching the same material.

Much learning that takes place at work does not have the clear goals of apprenticeship. Such would be the case where practising professionals continue to expand their knowledge through their day-to-day work. Gear, McIntosh and Squires (1994) have studied this type of learning and found that whilst on reflection participants in the study believed that they had learnt a lot this way, they were largely unaware of it until it was brought to their attention. Such learning mostly happens without clear intentions or overt effort, but can nevertheless make an important contribution to professional knowledge as this lawyer remarks.

> All through my career I have been engaged in informal learning without being aware of it, what you [researchers] call informal learning ... Until you actually sit down and think about the informal learning process, you don't realise how much you actually do ... it's not something you give any thought to at the time you're doing it, it just seems to happen ... If I come across something I haven't come across before, I can ask [a colleague] because she has been around for a long time and has the expertise, and say 'I haven't come across this before' and chat to her. Now that can cut down on 2 or 3 hours research. Now if I do that on other things as well, well I may just save some time there. And I might find out another bit of information which I wasn't looking for. So, you obviously can't sit all day chatting to people, but it's important to have exchanges with people, to have room for that, not just purely work things. And sometimes you may get a little bit extra out of somebody.
> (Gear, McIntosh & Squires 1994: 46)

Taking implicit learning in a slightly different direction Reber (cited by Eraut, 2000: 12), has described the 'acquisition of knowledge independently of conscious attempts to learn and the absence of explicit knowledge about what was learned'. This line of thought is supported by experimental evidence, mainly relating to artificial grammars and has more to do with the way in which people make subliminal connections by 'seeing' patterns or structure in a visual array without being consciously aware of them. A more everyday example would be the solution to a crossword clue just coming to mind, rather than being worked out. It is possible that these sorts of unconscious processes may help in language acquisition or in acquiring intuitive feelings about situations or other people. Clues are garnered and meaningful connections made at a level of thought that occurs without awareness.

Learning can also be the incidental by product of an activity in which the acquisition of knowledge is not the purpose of the activity yet is clearly the result of it, for example learning advocacy skills and gaining IT knowledge through involvement in community action (Cullen, Batterbury, Foresti, Lyons & Stern, 2000). Finally, we are all aware that a considerable amount of learning may be achieved when informally pursuing an interest or hobby. Gorard, Fevre, Rees, Furlong and Renold (1998) showed how considerable DIY expertise can be achieved in this way, as this participant in their study describes.

> Read it up, oh that's the way to do it ... I ordered a bricklaying book and read it ... with plastering now, a friend of mine is in the library and she got me a book, so ... if I got to do a job I'm not quite sure [about] I get a book and read it up and say 'oh well' this is the way. (p. 12)

Bringing together such diverse examples of adult informal learning into a coherent conceptual framework presents a challenge. Becket and Hager (2002) propose the main characteristics ...

– organic/holistic
– contextual
– (arising) in situations where learning is not the main aim
– activity and experience-based
– activated by individual learners rather than by teachers/trainers
– often collaborative/collegial.

When it comes to analysing actual examples of informal learning, its shifting, dynamic nature becomes clear (Garrick, 1998). Becket and Hager explain part of the difficulty when they point out that most adult learning takes place chaotically in 'the swamp' of everyday experience. Arnott, Fell and Bouson (2001) amply illustrate this in a study of 18 farmers and pastoralists in Northern Australia and how they went about making changes as they experimented with innovations such as growing watermalons, new crop rotations or entering the tourist market. Their study clearly illustrates both a mix of Beckett and Hagger's characteristics and the difficulty of pigeon-holing real-life learning into distinctive types.

In the swamp: informal learning at the cutting edge of knowledge

For the most part, learning theories are concerned with the dissemination of knowledge; how it is passed from one source to another. Little is known about how knowledge might actually be advanced into new areas, finding out what is *not* known rather than learning what already is known. In this respect informal learning where children may be trying to grasp a concept, under their own steam, may have parallels with those who are operating at the cutting edge of knowledge.

As we have seen, much informal learning is quite chaotic. Its products are often intangible, its processes obscure, its progress piecemeal. There are false starts, unrelated bits and pieces picked up, interests followed and discarded, sometimes to be taken up again, sometimes not. All this also accords with very advanced learning sometimes associated with scientific discovery, the early stages in crafting a novel, composing a piece of music or coming up with a solution to a technical problem. The following description by Watson of the discovery of the structure of DNA illustrates informal learning at this level (Watson, 1968).

In 1953 the scientific journal *Nature* published a groundbreaking article by Francis Crick and James Watson in which they presented their discovery of the double helical structure of the chemicals that make up DNA. Their work heralded a turning point in the sciences that study life and marked the beginning of a completely new direction in genetics. Their discovery was hailed as one of the major scientific events of the century and their inspiration recognized by Nobel prizes. In the typical style of learned journals, their findings, deliberately understated, were presented in dry, impersonal language and it was only in a much later publication that Watson let the world into some of the drama and human vagaries that had marked the two years in which he and Crick had puzzled over the nature of DNA.

In this later, anecdotal, version of the events leading up to the breakthrough *Nature* article, Watson reveals a very different view of science at the cutting edge. Using his notes, letters and diaries of the time Watson recreated the excitement, the rivalry, the emotions and personalities in a way which exposed the machinations of academic life and shed, in particular, a new light on the ways in which creative science is pursued. He revealed a social institution governed by personal likes and dislikes, chance and opportunism, prejudice and caprice; all a long way from the impersonal and cool detachment of the face of science presented in journals like *Nature*.

He also drops many interesting clues about the ways in which science operates as a cognitive system. The logical progression of reason by which the scientific method is often characterized, makes no appearance. Indeed at the breakthrough edge there can be no clear logical way to proceed. Different groups working on the structure of DNA were doing different things, following up different leads; sometimes sharing, but often guarding the information and clues which their work revealed. No one knew which direction was forward, no one knew which information was vital and which incidental, even the possibility that a definitive answer to their question existed, had to be assumed. Crick and Watson, as the other scientists working on the same problem, were very much at sea in a confusing, multifaceted situation with no clear route forward to where they wanted to go.

In the context of cutting-edge science Crick and Watson appear as huge intellects cutting paths of understanding through unknown territory, yet placed a little closer to home, they were simply people learning effectively in a situation of great uncertainty. How did they do it? Clearly they thought a lot about what they wanted to know. But Watson's account makes it plain that this thinking was not always directed and purposeful. He describes his daydreams of receiving a Nobel prize, his daydreams of how a breakthrough will feel, rather than the actualities of how it will occur. Sometimes he prefers not to think too hard about what he is doing, fearful of spotting the cracks in his own arguments, he puts off work, avoids things that he believes will be too difficult or that will necessitate too much hard work. Yet his subject is never far from his mind, in the cinema, on the train, at social occasions it seems that he returns to it over and over again.

Watson and Crick were collaborators, exchanging their thoughts, criticizing each other, making suggestions, asking more questions. They were, however, not alone in wanting to discover the structure of DNA. Other scientists working on the same problem were often more their rivals than their colleagues. Snippets of information came their way from various, not always wholly legitimate sources. These snippets had to be pondered over, judged, discarded or incorporated as Watson and Crick saw fit.

Watson uses the term 'play' to describe the endless fiddling around the problem. When there was not enough to go on to be purposeful, play kept the problem moving. At another time, Watson describes Crick as 'popping out' with ideas, partly based on his own thoughts and partly on an approach more to do with the person to whom he was speaking. Over and over again he makes reference to conversations, very often socially based conversations over meals and drinks. Sometimes these are seen as opportunistic chances to tap into someone else's ideas or to air their own, but sometimes just conversation of a wholly casual kind.

On a number of occasions Watson describes following up hunches, feelings and ideas unsupported by evidence. He acts on intuition, such as 'something was not right' or insists on pursuing a certain line of inquiry although 'I knew none of my reasons held water'. On the other hand pertinent evidence from a German scientist was dismissed, more or less out of hand, for what were then political reasons.

Watson's account makes it clear that for long periods of time the problem remained essentially static either because it was not being worked on or because the work that was being done was leading nowhere. On some occasions the false starts were their own fault as on the occasion when Watson incorrectly remembered the water content of some DNA samples and he and Crick spent considerable time working with this misinformation. For at least one whole year it appeared that no progress whatsoever was made, 'we still remained stuck at the same place we were twelve months before' (p. 121). Both drift off into other avenues of work and it seems as if DNA research has simply reached an unsuccessful standstill. Strangely enough though, Watson later attributes considerable meaning to the periods of doing and achieving nothing, 'much of our success was due to the long uneventful periods when we walked among the colleges or unobtrusively read the new books that came into Heffer's Bookstore' (p. 157).

Moving on

The sum of these, in many ways diverse, approaches to child and adult informal learning is to leave us with a heap of clues about informal learning rather than an overarching picture of how it works. At a basic level however, it is possible to distil what we have described into three main strands. The first of these is goal-directed learning where the individual sets out with the explicit purpose of pursuing a piece of knowledge so that what is being learned is plain to see. We can see this across the lifespan: babies exploring the physical environment, young children asking questions, older children working out computer procedures or driven by the real-life necessity of calculating money transactions correctly in the marketplace or, in the case of adults, pursuing an interest or hobby in some depth.

Secondly, there is learning which is incidental to the main activity at hand. For children this would include learning through play or when a parent shares a number rhyme with them, during shopping trips or travelling. For adults incidental learning occurs at home or at work, for example picking up snippets of information from a colleague during a casual chat, watching television or in DIY activities. While much of this learning might pass unnoticed it is at least feasible for a keen observer to see opportunities for such learning as they occur.

The third, implicit kind of learning occurs with little if any awareness. It appears that the brain processes information, organizes and reorganizes it subconsciously and then presents it at the conscious level. Such implicit learning has long been recognized but only in relation to socialization, the acquisition of cultural habits, mores, attitudes, values and behaviour patterns. There is now however an emerging interest in extending it into the cognitive domain and it may be that such learning plays a role even at the highest levels of intellectual achievement as we saw above in relation to the discovery of the structure of DNA.

Whilst theoretically these categories, implicit, incidental and goal directed, can be useful as a starting point in understanding informal learning processes, it is much harder to look at a child engaged in an activity and define what they are doing in such terms. For one thing, these categories are very often interwoven rather than separate from one another. Learning of all three types blend into each other and contribute variously to the same subject matter, once again reinforcing the view that informal learning does not hold any certain characteristics by which it can be reliably and consistently pinned down. There is however one feature which stands out, particularly as it contrasts with the important body of Vygotskian thinking about how children learn, and that is the degree to which informal learning is a learner-led activity. This feature cuts across the three categories above, being pertinent to all three, regardless of the levels of awareness which accompany learning.

The other important point about informal learning is precisely its lack of firm characteristics. Different ages, subject matters, levels of awareness, variation in inputs and assistance mean that, for the researcher, no two examples of informal learning seem to be the same. We need to accept the chameleon-like qualities of informal learning as one of its major strengths. For the learner it means that informal learning can take place in myriad ways in virtually all circumstances and subject matters. Its infinite adaptation allows informal learning to be an ongoing part of life; something which people do naturally and at which, perhaps, children excel. We will carry these lines of thought forward to the coming chapters on informal learning in childhood.

Informal learning is part of life and while people are living they are quite possibly learning, at some level, all or most of the time. It is therefore no mean task, to say the least, to distinguish when children are learning or precisely what they are learning. As Tudge, Hogan, Lee, Tammeveski, Meltsas, Kulakova, Snezhkova and Putnam (1988: 82) put it 'Children may learn no matter what activity they are engaged in.' However, within the context of home education we do not simply need to know that some kind of learning is taking place as it might be with preschool children and adults. If informal learning is to replace the school curriculum for ten years or so then what is learned is of paramount importance. In the next chapter we consider the type of informal learning opportunities open to children and the subject matter available to them.

Chapter 4

The informal curriculum

In the previous chapter we discussed the extent to which existing research and theory can shed light on the working practice of informal education. These theories are largely concentrated on building overarching concepts to explain how informal learning takes place. Our aim in this and the following chapter is to draw closer to children's informal learning by considering the more specific questions of what children learn and how they accomplish this within the context of their day-to-day lives. In this chapter we set out to explore how what is learnt informally at home and in the wider community can, at least up to the early secondary school years, cover much the same subject matter as formal learning in school.

In Chapter 3 we mentioned the socio-cultural theories of Super and Harkness (1982, 1986) and Cole (1998) who propose that very early learning, often termed as socialization, takes place quite naturally within families. From birth children in their developmental niche, are surrounded by a family and a society which operate in certain ways to reach certain ends. This creates adult behaviour patterns which influence how babies are treated and in this way children are caught up in their culture from the first days of their lives onwards. Cole's example concentrates on sleeping patterns but is easily extended to other forms of social behaviour. In fact, we accept very readily that children will learn sleeping patterns, eating patterns, basic self care, the household routine, language, little jobs like feeding the budgie and so on simply through being in the physical place and social context where these things happen. Cole sees this learning as a collaboration between family, community and newborn child to accept the new member of the family as someone like us who does what we do because what matters to us matters to them. In some societies children continue to learn, and only ever learn, in this way. However, as children get older the efficacy of this type of learning tends to be overlooked in technologically sophisticated societies where education is seen as a cognitive rather than a practical enterprise. This may be prematurely dismissive when we consider some of the expectations attached to children in non literate societies. The intellectual demands on them may be as strenuous as those required of learners in post-industrial societies and include complex knowledge in a number of fields such as myths and history, genealogies, religious and kinship rules as well as a range of skills and practical knowledge in topology, weaving, hunting, farming, animal husbandry, fishing, building, music, dance, etc. (Jahoda & Lewis, 1988).

Our contention is simply that the niche can continue to foster learning of both a social and a cognitive nature well beyond the age of five when as a society we assume that formal learning needs to take over. The social and physical environment which forms the learning context for these earliest experiences can continue to provide what we have termed the informal curriculum. In other words, the informal curriculum refers to the things which children learn when their learning is not deliberately structured or managed by an external agent but is brought about by a combination of social and environmental influences.

Super and Harkness (1982, 1986) argue that the developmental niche is created through parental behaviour which occurs in accordance with their values, beliefs and practical needs, rather than with any direct intention of teaching babies anything specific. For children who continue to be educated informally, what they learn is simply an extension of this. Children learning in this way do not think of themselves as 'learning' in the sense that they do in school. Nor do their parents think of themselves as teaching. People just live and learning is part of that. This is completely at odds with the professional belief that cultural knowledge needs to be harnessed and pre-digested within a set instructional framework before being presented to children. The idea that such knowledge can be picked up haphazardly in the chaos of everyday existence or left to the whim of child interest is almost laughable. Yet the chaotic nature of the informal curriculum does not appear to be a barrier to children organizing it into a coherent body of knowledge. In fact, in some ways it may be an advantage because rather than presenting knowledge in neat packages the informal curriculum forces learners to become actively engaged with their information, to work with it, move it around, juggle ideas and resolve contradictions far more so than in formalized learning. In her seminal study of children's thinking, Donaldson (1978) put forward the view that learning which derives from everyday life, which makes 'human sense' to children, may demand higher levels of cognitive engagement. In her study of young children's problem solving abilities she found that tasks that come embedded in day-to-day practical experience, as they are likely to be at home, elicited a higher order of thinking than those that are posed in more abstract terms or are contrived as they are in school. Even when knowledge outside the everyday domain is sought, this still makes 'human sense' because it stems from the child's own interest or curiosity. The point is that the real-life informal curriculum offers a consistently meaningful context. It is not a static thing contained in a series of educational folders. It is alive and dynamic.

It is our basic contention that the informal curriculum can operate without being intentionally orientated towards learning. However it is also the case that in our society, with its heavy emphasis on childhood education parents also contribute in more intentional ways, through conversation, by providing appropriate materials, books, computers, games and toys, arranging visits and so on. Parents respond to questions and requests for help, in relation to literacy and numeracy for example and by facilitating any particular interest that crops up. They suggest activities that might be of interest, and may involve children in everyday tasks such as shopping, going to the bank, helping a neighbour and cooking. There is however rarely any demand that something be learned in a particular way or to a particular time scale. That is left to the child. For most parents the only expectations are general ones; that their children will acquire an education sufficient for whatever they decide to do later on, whether that means starting on a formal course of learning in order to gain a qualification, finding paid employment or following up their interests in some other way.

How do parents describe the informal curriculum?

Parents naturally saw the informal curriculum in terms of the practical reality of their everyday lives; first referring to the world around their children including the influence of family activities and interests and secondly, in terms of interests that children had embarked on for themselves which, in some cases extended into considerable expertise. As we shall see, there is nothing special about the informal curriculum, it is what most children in school experience on a part-time basis. It is just that for children educated informally, *it's all there is*.

The everyday cultural curriculum

The everyday cultural curriculum consists of the commonly held ideas, knowledge and skills that help people operate within their environment. It surrounds us all the time and forms the natural learning curriculum for all pre-school children both at home and in the community. For example, Weinberger (1996) looking at the lives of pre-school children points out the considerable opportunities that there are for small children to become acquainted with different aspects of literacy simply through being with their parents or watching them in their day-to-day activities. This is equally the case for many other aspects of knowledge pertinent to everyday life. A child accompanying their parent to the shops, for instance, has the opportunity to become acquainted with aspects not only of literacy but also numeracy, economics, geography, social relations, technology, how to organize a simple trip, time-related concepts and perhaps many more. One parent outlined some of the learning opportunities encountered by her children through their everyday contact with life in their community.

> [They learn] how society works. They know how to look things up at the library, how the catalogue works, who to ask if they need something,

where to go, what to do. You have to pay to park the car. There are people in uniform. Are they a policeman or a parking inspector? They learn things about people too. They stand back and observe people in the shops and say things like, 'They weren't too interested in serving the customer were they?' They notice and comment on the shop assistants who say in one running stream: 'How-are-you-today-thanks-very-much-see-ya-later.' The children always notice that. Often because they are there and a lot of adults treat children as though they are not there, they can make some interesting observations. And also they notice the difference between the adults who treat children as people and those who brush them aside: Get out of the way!

Sometimes one of the children says something and I wonder where it came from. They just seem to absorb things by osmosis. Sometimes they are just around and overhear things in conversation, see things on T.V. We watch a lot of documentaries. [My husband] and I are both interested in history. Anything good that's going to be on about history – Australian history, English history, military history – we want to watch … So I think a lot of learning just happens without you being aware of it. I keep a record, a rough record of what we do each day but so often I'm aware there's lots going on that isn't written down. (5)

Everyday life offers virtually unlimited opportunities to read, write, tell the time, do simple sums, estimate quantities, distance, time, articulate ideas and to engage with society and gain insights into how it functions. Simple activities like catching a bus, going to the doctor or the swimming pool, visiting a park or a museum allow children to pick up practical skills and to come to understand some of the ways in which society organizes itself and operates. Children who are out and about with their parents, involved in the running of the household and with the lives of adults will have ample opportunity to come into contact with and build their understanding of how society works. Even at home with their families the influences of the wider society permeate: where the money comes from, what to do when something breaks down, putting out the rubbish, mail being delivered, what is on television, newspapers, magazines and other written material, the internet, advertising, films and so on.

As one parent pointed out children are highly, if not innately, motivated to become like the people around them. Engagement with the informal curriculum offers a route to precisely that.

Children want to be grown up and they want to be accepted into the community. They don't want to be weird and different and not like the people around them. It's this natural kind of social thing we've all got. Fundamentally you want to be able to talk to the people around you. You want to have your ideas accepted as being reasonable and able to communicate and have a part to play. For children that community is their family and then it becomes the extended family and then it becomes the local community and then it becomes the wider world. The very first experience they have of that is wanting to be like their Mum and wanting to be like their Dad and possibly like their older siblings. Babies want to talk because you talk to them … all of a sudden you are having a conversation. (3)

Parents saw this engagement with the world around them, not just as a background to learning but as an essential aspect of the informal curriculum.

She doesn't seem worse off than any other child who goes to school for all those hours every day. She seems to pick up the same information, the same necessary information, survival stuff, social stuff … (24)

[They both] see the whole world as a place to learn (18)

[Learning] is just part of her life and she plods along and each time she picks something up and takes it in. And she does like we were saying before, where did she get that from? How does she know that? (24)

I think that they are processing information all the time and working out what it means in reality to them. (16)

I think they learn life skills through living at home; they all do chores as well (20)

The extent to which children become directly involved with or make use of this common knowledge increases naturally as they get older. They run errands or spend their pocket money, ask for information from a shop assistant, plan a simple journey, read a large variety of different materials from advertising to literature and so on. They can also take on some adult type responsibilities.

[He] is going to London for his birthday, we are going to spend the night and the day and do what he wants to do. He has to learn to book the hotel, to sort out the tourist information and he is now sorting out the itinerary so that when we get there he's going to know what we are going to do, when we are going to do it and that is going to carry on with him. That is considered to be a leisure occupation but he's going to learn to do this and it's going to carry on as he gets older. (18)

When she was ten she paid for a two week trip interstate, down to Melbourne in Victoria where my mother lives because she wanted to go on a holiday and she wanted to do it without her family and she wanted to visit her grandmother and she discovered that the ticket was only a $100 each way and she could buy one on the internet. So, over a period of 10 months she saved up $200 and bought herself a return plane ticket and she went to Melbourne for two weeks. [Now, aged nearly 14] she's going to America at the end of this year. Things scale up as they get older. (3)

Yet despite, or even because of this clear engagement with the informal curriculum the lines between simply living and learning are very blurred even for those closest to the process. Because much of the understanding being acquired is considered so commonplace and is implicitly or incidentally rather than explicitly gathered, it can be very difficult to spot learning taking place even for those involved in the situation. The following exchange shows how far the strongly articulated purpose and aims of formal education may be missing from the informal curriculum.

> The [Local Authority] guy who was doing the visits first came a few years ago and I decided that I was going to be completely hard line, I wasn't going to help him at all, so I said, 'We don't do anything. We just hang out.' And he said 'Well when your children do writing would they be doing it in exercise books or on loose paper?' and I said, 'They only do purposeful writing; they write letters and lists and stuff that they want to write' so he said, 'Well what about maths?' and I said, 'They get pocket money, we do cooking.' (26)

Anyone observing this kind of learning may simply feel that nothing of any consequence is happening; there is very little by which progress can be measured, certainly in the short term when the goals and strategies of formal education are no longer in place.

> To be honest they didn't really do things that I would call academic at all. … We did bits and pieces of craft stuff. If they got interested in something, they would read up about it. I read out loud quite a lot, most of it fiction but quite a lot of historical fiction and fiction with information in it. But most of the time they just hung out and played with friends. The only thing that I would say, I tended to describe to people that what we did with home education as being like summer holidays. Think what your kids do in the summer holidays and that's what we did most of the time. (26)

This young man, now in his early twenties and completing a PhD in computing science, remembered typical days from his childhood in rural Australia in the same vein.

> A typical day would have been, depending on what we wanted to do, we might have got up early to go ferreting or otherwise we would have slept in, got up a bit later, taken the dogs and gone down the creek. Often [my brother and I] wouldn't come back until it was late in the afternoon or

approaching dark. Often we'd take fruit or whatever with us. It also widely varied. Some days we'd hike up the hill over the other side there, head up there and spend the day chasing rabbits and stuff and other days we'd disappear and build cubbies. That would be a typical day. Often I would help [my mother] around the place, rounding up sheep or gardening or doing washing or milking goats, those sorts of things, wood collecting and splitting wood. [Also] around 10, 11 or 12 [years of age] there was a guy who we referred to as our adopted grandfather who was in his late 60s early 70s at the time and he would come out once a week and take us hunting and fishing or whatever the case would be. And just a lot of the hands on skills and knowledge he was able to pass on, whether it be how to tie a hook on the end of a fishing line or sharpening knives, he used to work as a meat inspector so things such as sharpening knives, filleting fish, hands on skills which you can certainly read about but it's far easier to have someone show you how it's done. (2)

In spite of the carefree nature of this lifestyle children are learning, and may be garnering all sorts of information of which even parents may not be aware.

It's interesting that when you go for informal learning you have to wonder what is taking the place of those routine hours and the set curriculum [in school] and I think it's very much what is in the environment and I think a great part of that is what the parents give out in terms of their, maybe as [my partner] says, interests, passions but also just their own basic skills. So without knowing it, it might be your level of housekeeping the children are learning most from. (4)

Parental interests

Parents themselves contributed to the cultural curriculum in various ways. All the families made deliberate efforts to take children out, to introduce them to things and activities, to offer them opportunities and to actively help them to become acquainted with the life around them. To this extent, families are deliberately creating environments of stimulation and interest.

I took them to home-educating events and took them to museums and places of interest and answered their questions and I provided entertainment, playing games with them. (26)

I might introduce things, things are introduced, things are put in their path, they are never just left in limbo with nothing happening around them. (18)

I am guiding her and I am reading to her. (24)

Me or my partner will think, 'let's get on this band wagon and give them a bit of education here'. (21)

I do think that to a certain extent parents have to put their children into certain situations, certain environments in which they can learn. (17)

Another way in which parents and other family members contribute to the informal curriculum is through the family environment created by their own work, interests, beliefs and life styles.

[My daughter] is a musician and an artist; she is following very much in my footsteps ... I could spend 12 hours a day with my daughter doing what she wants to do because that is what I want to do as well – that's the music and the art. (21)

The way our family operates is um ... We are all passionately interested in knowledge. We all like books, we like movies, we like talking books, we like computers. If there is a good documentary on, everybody wants to come and watch it. It's not compulsory or anything. If there's something on at 7.30 that looks good, everybody turns up to watch it ... They all learn from each other. Thomas knows a lot about astronomy. It's not directly his interest but he knows because ... he's here when Kevin [his elder brother] is talking about it. He might be playing Lego on the floor but he hears the conversation and similarly, Kevin has very little interest in war history but he knows things about it because he's heard conversations and overheard documentaries that Thomas and [my husband] have watched and so on ...
  The boys learn different things from different people. [My husband's] interested in shares and military history. I'm interested in the kings and queens, Australian history. Just in the conversation between the boys and ourselves we cover different things. We talk about what we've been reading or articles we've seen in the newspaper, programmes we've watched, feelings we've had. They go and visit Grandma and Granddad and learn different things from them. They learn things from neighbours. One of our neighbours is a fisherman and knows things about cars, handyman stuff – the kinds of things the boys are never exposed to here. In conversation with these people they pick up different things ...
  I'm more or less a facilitator. Driving to the library and just being here and talking about things. A lot of our learning is just conversation. I provide materials, resources, help with research, discuss what they are reading and what I am reading, watch documentaries with them, watch movies, have stimulating conversations, listen a lot and answer a lot of questions. I am interested in what they are doing and they are interested in what I do also. I do a bit of writing and editing and layout work on a magazine. Kevin and Robert like to read a lot of what I write and comment

on it as well as giving page-layout suggestions and so on. Sometimes I follow their advice, sometimes I don't. Sometimes they follow my advice, sometimes they don't. (5)

The culture around you is the most important thing. I was very confident about them being literary and probably musical, artistic and intellectual because that is the culture of our house. There's a lot of that stuff happening all the time. I thought if I didn't do anything with them ever it would just be, if I didn't do any lessons with them, they would just be unable to survive in that environment without becoming at least one of those things … (1)

The following example shows how children might take on the interests of their parents almost as informal apprentices.

[He] loves computers. He has an affinity with the logic and the predictability of computers, in the way they work. His father's a computer programmer. His uncle's a computer programmer. His other uncle's a graphic designer for a games company. He got a job when he was 12 as a basketball referee so that he could save up money to buy a computer which he did. It cost him $1000. He took nearly two years to save it up. Now he's getting a bigger job so he can buy a bigger, better computer. He's applying for a job at a supermarket. He does a lot of computer support within the family. The family have stopped calling my husband and have started calling my son. He builds computers for people like they say I want a 1.2 GHz computer with 512 megabytes of RAM and a 'this' and a 'that'. He'll order all the components and put it all together because that will work out a couple of hundred dollars cheaper and he'll charge $50 or something for that. He's learning Java [script] so he's writing his own programs and his little game engines, like little Packman things that run around the screen. And he plays a lot of games, strategy games and shooting games and simulation games like Sim City and things like that.
[*Interviewer*: Does he discuss computing with his Dad?]
I don't know that discuss is the right word. He asks his Dad when he gets stuck … He's picked up work at my husband's company. They have casual work and they often have a bunch of old technology which they get him to come in and catalogue and test what works and what doesn't and then they donate all the good stuff to charity and junk the rest. It's leading him in different directions …

[His interest] would have been hard to avoid it because we've always had computers and they've always been interested in what we do. So his very earliest days were spent on the breast while I'm trying to type one handed and there's the mouse and learning to use the mouse, playing the early games and rapidly getting bored with the early games and wanting to play the same games that daddy plays … He's always thought far beyond his age, so he got bored with [child games] quite rapidly and just wanted to get into adult games to play what [his father] played. They are quite complicated. They wallop my butt because I don't have time to sit down and develop the skills. I have to team up with my husband even to stand a chance against them ...

[His sister's] exposure to computers has been just the same, but what she ends up doing with them is very different. She's also quite artistic and has always been into drawing and painting and things like that. Where she's ended up now at nearly 14 – she uses Photoshop and Design which are desktop publishing packages. She helps me on the [home education] magazine. Some of the drawings in the magazine have actually been processed and inked by her. She's doing work that is practically of professional standard in some very specific areas. But it's artistic. She's never been interested in programming. It's all been design stuff. She's created a few websites in the past. She was breeding guinea pigs for a couple of years to earn money, breeding and selling guinea pigs. She created a website for that. She had photographs of all the guinea pigs and descriptions about them. (3)

Children's interests

The last example given above, shows how different children can take different things from the same environment and how the same background can nurture different learning trajectories. This streak of individualism could be seen directing the learning of informally educated children from the earliest years onwards, taking them beyond the immediate environment and introducing them to knowledge drawn from other sources. In our culture, expanding knowledge beyond basic requirements is integral to being educated. Children in school mostly rely on the curriculum to select such knowledge. At home, parents expected and relied to a considerable extent on children following up and learning from their own interests. In the early years it often seemed to be a case of being imaginative and pro-active in exploring or combining the information and ideas around them as these parents describe:

The two boys built a fort thing when they were 6 or 7. They spent two years on it. Though they couldn't read or write they knew all about the US Civil War. Now they read all about the battles. They recreate things they find out about, build things and draw things and different people. He goes outside to recreate and 'live' things, such as digging holes for a rock thrower. (11)

Lego is a huge interest. He has quite a bit of Lego. It's what he does with it. First he gets books of aircraft, military or civilian, not models but actual pictures and he models them from Lego. No one tells him to make 3D models of different aircraft and so on. He models them and compares them back to the picture and if he likes them he photographs them and puts them in his collection. And these are not making them from predetermined designs, but from a photograph he's seen some place and decides to model that particular plane. (8)

Computers are a great example I think. Never at any stage have we made a conscious effort to teach the children how to use the computer. Somehow they know. Some of their knowledge exceeds mine because ... they've got time to play with it and children seem less hesitant than adults about clicking on things and seeing what happens. [One of them] has recently learned how to produce Power Point shows and use Power Point for animation. He is doing some pretty incredible stuff with it. [His older brother] showed him some things [and his other brother] showed him some more. [He] sat beside them whilst they were working and he has experimented. I haven't taught him anything to do with that – in fact he knows more about it than I do. (5)

He has learned everything from a hole in the ground, he dug a hole in his garden and it became a 'mine' and [my son] was part of the FFJC Mining Company and it moved on and on and on and it got terribly sophisticated. We were getting certificates of continuing professional development through the post from it and telephone lists and stuff and all this really a huge amount of effort and thought. His whole life was around this mine. When it was a rainy day he'd go in and do office work. (23)

Interests flowed, apparently quite naturally, as children began to explore avenues which took them beyond their everyday experiences. Sometimes it was possible to trace the course of interests as one thing led to another.

She'll be doing a drawing and then think, 'it would be good if I made it in clay' ... she'll be working on several strands at the same time, but she's doing these fantasy drawings and she decided to do them in colour and then that led to an oil painting and that led to getting interested in how other people have used oil through the ages, so history of art. (21)

Overall, the range of interests was very broad with animals, computers, strategy games, reading and writing, art, music, practical skills, languages and sciences all represented. Often parents struggled to see just where an interest had sprung from; confounding the fear expressed by some people that children would necessarily be restricted by the knowledge or lives of their own household.

Mother: I don't know where the interest in astronomy came from. It just cropped up and we've followed his interest. Even [his] Grandma looks out for newspaper articles about the planets, new ones that have been discovered. In some ways [his brother's] interest in military history seems to have been inherited from [my husband] and you might think that [he] might have started it, but it just seemed to start on its own. [My husband] was delighted that he got interested and just encouraged it. But I don't think he actually introduced him to it. Did you?

Father: No. One day he just found my old soldiers and things out in the garage. He knew exactly what to do with them and what they were about.

Older brother: When he started, the soldiers had stereos in the Wild West.

Father: Well, he may have had one of them having a stereo in the Wild West but it became more historically accurate as he went on ...

Mother: [Now] he's particularly interested in the American Civil War. He'll be very interested in a particular thing for a space of time, then he'll move on. It doesn't mean he's necessarily finished with that. He generally comes back to it. One week it will be pirates. He can tell you all about Anne Bonny and Elizabeth Reed – the female pirates. Another week it'll be the Civil War or the American War of Independence, or it could be World War Two or World War One ... the Napoleonic Wars. (5) He was fascinated by Japan. We don't really know where it comes from. He's interested in all the Pokemon stuff. He was interested in Japan before that because he collected china dolls for a while. There has been something about Japanese things that have fascinated him. Again we don't really know why or where it comes from because I haven't tried to dig about in those kind of things. My feeling has been that if that is what you are fascinated in – great! So he started learning Japanese off tapes but the tapes were very poor. We tried very hard to get somebody who was Japanese to teach him but we couldn't find anybody here out in West Cork. We didn't manage to get down that route, but I bought him lots of stuff about Japan, read him books about Japan, played games about Japan, sailing to Japan and what happened there but without any educational intent, just with the intent of having fun. I bought him magazines with educational intent to support his interest. But those would have been about Pokemon things and video games, things that he's interested in. I bought him any books on Japan I could get, [one] about a guy hitch-hiking around Japan. He read those so he reads to a very high level. He read a book by Carey, a Booker winner. He read that all the way through because it was about Japan. ... [He] is still into Japan but the thing he's been engrossed in over the past 18 months is music really. (1)

How far children went in following these interests was up to them. Although parents were keen to support their children's interest, initiation and impetus were provided by the child and child expertise frequently went well beyond the parent's knowledge or capability. One consequence of this choice and control was that an interest could be taken up, pursued for as long as desired or dropped at any point. Some children were described as single minded and wholly dedicated to their current causes.

> They are more than hobbies to them, ruling passions almost. I would say that for [him] it is playing on-line games and strategy games on the computer and the magic cards. They are his ruling passions and they will last for several months, if not years, before they are replaced with another one and he won't want to do anything else except for those. (21)

> He is very, very single minded in his own interests and doesn't really pay a great deal of attention to what other people are doing. (20)

> He follows this very narrow path of interest. He's very focused. At the moment it's the PlayStation, since Christmas that's his main thing. (15)

At other times children dipped in and out of interests or maintained a more general, wider focus.

> [She] is interested in everything you can think of. She does ballet and tap and now Karate as well and she wants to do gymnastics. She's interested in space and in learning languages and she wants to be able to knit and just to do everything. (25)

> She always had a really wide range of things that she enjoyed: physical and intellectual. (16)

> He became interested in music so I taught him an amount on the piano . And then he kind of got a bit bored with the piano and he then decided electronics was the thing so he went to Dick Smith [Electronics Retail Chain Store] and got all these electronic kits and spent the next 6 months putting together all the electrical wiring. He's actually done a large amount of the electrical wiring in here. We're on a 12 volt system. (2)

On the face of it many of children's pursuits are not at all 'educational' in the school sense. Rather they appear recreational, what children might do outside school. Yet whether 'educational' or not, these interests allow children to explore a topic at length, research, problem solve, persevere and develop a sense of mastery which, as well as providing them with some unusual knowledge, also helps develop the skills and concentration which can be applied to later learning or study.

> She now has the skills to take a fleece and spin it and dye it and go right through to the finished article. (16)

She got an origami book and taught herself to do everything in that book. Neither of us could do most of the things that she did. (15)

During the course of playing you're remembering what cards other people are playing because each card has its own set of rules so you have to see what other people are playing and what they are going to attack you with and then you have to understand your own cards and decide which ones are going to interact with which other ones and its just very complicated so there must be a huge amount of learning going on. It's very strategic. (21)

My son's current obsession is Yu-Gi-Oh cards which is just cards like Pokemon but more advanced and in actual fact what Yu-Gi-Oh has actually done for him is that it has improved his English reading, because there is tons to read and really complicated words, it's improved that, it has made him think about looking after things, it's made him think about collecting things, he's been looking at the art on the cards. When you start thinking about it he has done so much through having these cards and yet I had this woman from an LEA saying, 'Well I don't know how it works for you, but I would consider myself to be totally irresponsible if I just allowed my son to play with Yu-Gi-Oh cards all day.' (23)

Is the informal curriculum sufficient?

If children are in control of their own learning and free to follow whatever interests them, pursue it obsessively or drop it at will, how can one be sure they will obtain an education which will equip them to enter either formal education or employment at some future stage? If their time and energy are devoted single mindedly to just one or two subjects, how can this compensate for missing out on the broad scope of subjects in the National Curriculum? Some parents commented on the narrow focus of their children's interests and on the gaps in knowledge which simply following a passion might leave.

I don't know about older than my son, who is nine, but certainly at his age and a bit younger, they seem to be obsessed by something. If you were to walk into the house and spend a day in the house you would think, if you came from that school mindset: 'My God does he just do this all day?' (23)

There must be alarming gaps. I sometimes think of all the hours that school children spend in classes, they must be there when lots of information is given to them, how much they retain I don't know, but at least they have been told it. My kids haven't heard, I would love to have told them but they never asked. (21)

Balancing this was the view that any 'gaps' were of a transitory nature and would, if they constituted essential knowledge, be filled in given time:

> This is the funny thing about autonomous education that I find, that you have these massive peaks in certain areas and then what appear to be gaps in other areas but they do fill in eventually of their own accord don't they? Over time it becomes a sort of whole 'balanced curriculum' it does over time fill itself out, but because they are doing education by following their interests you get these big pushes forward in certain aspects. (23)

Parents themselves were often ambiguous on the question of how much they felt able to rely on the informal curriculum. Nearly all of the parents interviewed stressed the desire, or even the need, that learning should be child led, following up the child's interests. Yet they also often had firm ideas about what they wanted their children to learn and often worried about whether this was being adequately achieved. The following parent describes in detail this common dilemma.

> [We tell our] friends, 'No we are not going to teach them physics because we believe they will have the skills to learn it when and if they need it' ... So it's very hard when we have expounded this informal system to other people – it's very hard for us to turn round and say, ok, today we'd like you to sit at the table and do 20 minutes writing. You've really hung yourself ... When you don't have a set curriculum set out for learning you've removed that and almost everything in the environment is available to the children and different children will respond to different elements of it. This comes with a big question mark because I do have moments of extreme anxiety about would it not be better if we just got a book out and make sure they cover this.
>
> All our friends have their 3 o'clock in the morning doubts. I suppose there's this business of having to go forward. We've adopted a very informal style – trusting in the child's own ability to learn. Now I can look at some home-educated children who are 16 and 14 and are doing really well and I can say ok I have to hold on to that trust. Neither myself nor [my partner] would let me turn around tomorrow and become all formal about it. But the urge is there and at the moment we are experiencing [one of our daughter's] peer group making the transition to secondary school. So there's a lot of choice going on. Parents are choosing the schools and in a way I recognize that for what it is. Which is a false sense of control so they will think that choosing this above that school they will have gotten a better package. I don't believe that. I want the girls to stay in control of their own destiny if you like. Where I question it is when perhaps they aren't meeting the targets that are there in the school world and the most visible one for me would perhaps be writing. So I'm not worried about the

girls' curriculum or body of knowledge being completely different from that in school because that's all a curriculum or syllabus is. Somebody has decided these are the things a child should learn. I don't believe in that. But I do believe in them having skills and being in a position to make real choices about their careers and their life.

So I suppose you can't prove it until you've proved it. We've come across this in our discussions before. You can't rest upon anybody else. If you take a child who's been through school and who then is failing in some obvious fashion, the parent can be absolved because the school system has let them down whereas there's nobody else to blame – everybody is going to say 'What did you expect?'

... I think you've got the two basics from my point of view. One is a strong belief that it works and great excitement at being alongside someone who is doing it. But on the other hand, perhaps because of my own education and the culture we're in, there is a strong reliance on the formal, and anxieties when we're not getting there. So I can talk to another home education parent who's worrying about lack of spelling or something in one of their children and I can be really supportive and positive because I don't see it as a problem for them. But when it comes home and there's no writing going or the quality of writing that my girls would be capable of compared with a school child of that age would make me cringe. So that's where the paradox comes in. ... [What the children have is] freedom to think and time to pursue your own things. If I don't get around to formally finding [my other daughter] the maths workbook that she could do with now that would give her progress during the next two weeks, at least I'm not putting her on the bus to school and occupying her time in a completely pointless way. ... (4)

Some parents set subject matter aside and concentrated on the thinking and learning skills which their children were acquiring, referring to intellectual rather than practical skills; personal attributes and experience rather than knowledge. This could be summed up as the ability to think in some depth on a topic, to know how to approach, explore and find out more about a subject and to have the confidence, problem solving abilities and personal wherewithal to go wherever their future interests might take them.

I feel that if we are teaching them anything, we are teaching them how to think, how to actually work stuff out, that's the most valuable skill that you can get good at ... thinking skills ... How to think, how to work out, how to envisage ... that you can apply to anything. (19)

I don't know the capital of Madagascar but I know where the globe is. And so I think they've got all the basics that you would need or as near as much as I have and I think if they had trouble they would ask somebody or they would go and find it out in a book. They'd definitely have the confidence to do it. The main thing about them would be the confidence in their own ability. ... just being able to sort out anything they need to sort it out. (1)

I think knowing how to research, getting books out of the library, talking to people who have got similar interests, or going on workshops, once you've done it in one thing, then if you are interested in another thing you know how to go about finding out or you're not shy to ask. ... I think having a special interest and having time to pursue it does help with your confidence ... I hope that when they get to 16, 17, 18 they'll be better prepared to make decisions about higher education and careers and so on than I was, when I was that age through being able to spend their time more freely as children. (20)

This is probably the way his life will continue to go. He probably won't consider that he needs to hesitate before he jumps in and, it sounds dangerous as if they've got no cares at all, but of course they have, of course they learn to be cautious but they don't learn those personal boundaries that make people say I don't know whether I can do that, they don't learn those. I can see that carrying on, feeling able to do and not being restricted. (18)

Entering formal education

Compared to the careful way in which the curriculum is presented in school, the chaotic nature of input from everyday cultural knowledge and the individually led interests of children themselves, seem like a chancy combination. It nevertheless does seem that the informal curriculum is as good a preparation as any for moving into formal education. Children entered the formal system, either by going to school, college or university or by taking up home-based formal courses such as correspondence courses at around the GCSE (Year 11) level or later. Whenever this stage arrived for them personally, it seems that the young people themselves were able to decide on their own terms what and how they wanted to study and had both sufficient subject knowledge and study and personal skills to make the transition with apparent ease.

Basically what happened is that at fifteen she decided that she wanted to find out about chemistry and went to an evening class and her general knowledge and I guess her ability to learn, she hadn't had the previous ten years of doing science at school but it didn't seem to matter at all. (26)

She did nothing formal. She played outside and had lots of fun. She was seriously into piano and cello. That made me think. If you could find out what each child was good at, they would become experts whatever it was. It would give them confidence to learn. [My daughter] can play and sight read. People who play with her can see she's good. At fifteen she decided [to go to college] next year was Grade 11 [first year of college]. We were horrified but tried to be relaxed about it. Her plan was to do an adult ed. course for 18 weeks, to get up to Grade 10 level in maths. We shook our heads, remembering how she'd been [so negative about maths] but we took her. She got a High Achievement. She really worked hard to get it. (11)

He's completed four units at TAFE [Technical and Further Education]. It's adult education. It's mostly designed for adults who've dropped out of high school and are coming back to education. It's at Year 10 level. And there's an age limit on it so it's actually quite difficult getting him in because he was technically below the age limit. He really wanted to do the computing unit and the maths unit. The choice was his again but we went along to the orientation day and he did an assessment and they said his maths skills were pretty good and so he signed up for computers and then the next semester he signed up for maths which were the two he wanted to do. (3)

At eleven she came to TAFE with me to do weaving. My husband suggested I'd like to go. I thought I needed to do something with [her] so I suggested it and she just agreed. I just said: 'I'm going to do this. Are you going to come?' She said: 'If I like it, ok, if not I'll pull out like I did for Spanish.' TAFE needed numbers. They'd have loved more artistic people but they needed numbers and so she was able to enrol. But she was treated just like any of the adults. A girl of eleven in a course with her Mum! She was able to act like an adult. She never once said: 'I'm a kid. I can't manage this ...

At the start of this year they closed down the TAFE course. The teacher left to start a course at the uni. and we all enrolled there. They mentioned [my daughter] and there was a phone call in early February from the Head of the Art School, to bring [her] in and enrol her. The TAFE course counted as half a Diploma. The Diploma finishes at the end of this year. It's full time with nine hours face to face and studio time. And on Friday mornings there's a drawing class. They didn't know she was [now] fourteen and treated her like everyone else. I'm doing the course and he didn't even know we were related. We've done exhibitions, residencies and sold things. ... We went for five days on one residency. We set up looms and people came to talk to us. We had displays and sold things. She sold as much as me. We went on bush walks as well. After the Diploma she wants to go to College. The Diploma is the equivalent of 1½ years of a BA in Fine Art. But she wants to go to college! [Grade 11 and 12]. (11)

We never sat down with any of them and said what is it that you want to do in the future. With my son the need was there to learn how to weld so he did a welding course [at 13 he did a TAFE welding course for a framework that was needed at home]. He chatted to the chap who did the cleaning up afterwards [because] we had to find neighbours who were willing to take him there and bring him back. So he would often have to wait around in the evenings and got chatting to the chap who did the cleaning up. J. must have been talking to him at one point about not knowing what he wanted to do in the future and this chap said to him, his suggestion was whatever you plan to do in the future you need to know how to work a computer so why don't you do computing until you work out what you want to do. [He] came home saying he thought that was a pretty good idea so we pursued that and that's what led him to doing the TAFE course that led to the next TAFE course and suddenly in conversation with somebody he discovered that gave him credits for uni. so he went to the uni. and it's just gone on [to having just completed his PhD]. (2)

This book is not about demonstrating how much home-educated children can achieve academically. It is about exploring a viable and, for some or maybe many or most children, a different and more fulfilling way of becoming educated. The following example is given simply to show how an interest which begins informally early on, can be developed and can lead to outstanding achievement. It's not being hot-housed in the sense usually accorded to the term. It's hot-housing oneself because of a very high level of interest in a subject. If anything it demonstrates that children may be much more capable than we think if they are given a choice as to what to learn and control over their learning.

Computers had started to come in by the time he was thirteen. It wasn't a big thing early on but [he] fell in love with computers. He started designing his own model yachts. He learned computer programs to do it, design the yacht and then go and sail it which totally blew me away because I didn't understand anything of what he was doing. He's got a whole heap of things he designed when he was 12 or 13. And he thought nothing of it. And neither did I really until I looked back. He loved it. He spent all his time on that. Then aircraft started coming into that and he started making model planes. He still does. He's got a huge workshop where he's making helicopters. [When he was fifteen] we moved back down to Melbourne. Again, I didn't know what he was after. A lot of it, rockets, he started to make model rockets … rocket science. He started to become really interested. But I don't think at that stage that he even realised he could do anything professionally like that. It was, like way up here – he thought it would be way above him …

He expected to go to university and not TAFE [having spent two years in college and failed his university entrance examination]. It was a 2 year [Further Education] Diploma. His marks were so high that they held up his projects as examples of good work. He just was through the roof in that two years. With his score he went straight into the second year of a bachelor of aerospace degree. He's always been in the top six, the whole time. You need a [university entrance] score of 99/100 to get into it.

Now he's doing his second year of a PhD in aerospace engineering. He won an award last year for the most outstanding student of Level Four [Fourth Year Honours], both social and academic. Now he's designing his own model aircraft, he's a glider pilot and very highly involved in the gliding community. I went out to visit him and people were congratulating me on what a fine young man he was. I said to them it was nothing to do with me. He's always very shy.

He got into it because he always had a love of flying and unbeknown to you it grows. It was just always there. You see a book about it and pick it up. You pick it up and subconsciously you are attracted to it. He wasn't dialoguing with anyone about it, just reading books, loved to go to the space museum when he was in America. Anything to do with space. When we were in New York State we went to a museum when he was six and there was a cockpit of a Boeing. I've never seen a kid so happy in my life, sitting in that chair. (7)

Chapter 5

Engaging with the informal curriculum

In the previous chapter we showed how the everyday cultural world that surrounds children serves as a kind of informal curriculum from which children can acquire what they need to know to operate in society. It contains most of the knowledge that children in school are expected to learn, at least through to the secondary stage of education, but it is not harnessed, pre-digested and formalized as it needs to be in school. Most basic cultural knowledge is simply there for children to acquire piecemeal and haphazardly in their everyday lives. Further knowledge, outside the realm of everyday experience, is available through a variety of sources including family members and other people, the internet, books, the media, visits to places of interest and so on. However, the informal curriculum has to be more than just there. Children have to engage with it. In what follows we will try to explain how this engagement occurs.

Parents had generally given some thought to how their children learned but found it difficult to pin down the means involved; a problem also for researchers concerned with informal learning! So how did they describe their children's learning? We start at the implicit end of the informal learning dimension by considering learning that occurs when a child is apparently doing nothing, something most of us can relate to when we leave a problem to do something different and find that the solution simply comes to us, while we are thinking about something else. We then turn to learning through observation and conversation in which learning could be implicit or incidental, followed by self-directed learning, described in terms of intellectual search and exploration. Finally we look at the role of practice, necessary for the consolidation of knowledge and skills. Play, which we also believe to encompass enormous learning potential, is discussed separately in Chapter 7. A major problem is that informal learning is a fluid phenomenon; different forms of engagement overlap and interact with each other and constitute a dynamic and lively process. This may make informal learning hard to trace, but is also probably a key feature of why and how it is so effective.

Doing nothing

We all know that a problem we have encountered can be overcome if we take a break from it and do something else. In other words there is some kind of consolidation or processing going on at a subconscious level. Parents were often aware that their children appeared to have taken a leap forward in their learning for no explicable reason.

> She used to learn to play the violin, although she didn't do much practising, but every time she picked it up she was that little bit better. (24)

> [She] took up the cello when she was five and dropped it after about a year and then picked it up again when she was about eight. ... It certainly didn't seem to do her any harm, dropping it. ... [when she started again] she certainly wasn't like a beginner and in fact she didn't even seem to be where she had left it, she was a bit further ahead. (21)

> She liked the idea of reading but it didn't come together. At five she didn't read but she'd just pick out a word here and there. She made no progress for a whole year ... Then she wrote something down, it was really good compared with what she normally wrote. I sort of knew that something had changed. We had gone away for five weeks. When we went she couldn't read, when we came back she could. (14)

> I've noticed with anything that she does that she has to go away and assimilate it. It has to click through, stick ... And time. Sometimes that seems to be what makes it work for her, to take on board new things. When she had rollerblades, she was desperate for rollerblades and she got them and she couldn't do it. She did a little bit and I was really encouraging, 'It's really hard because it's brand new' but that was it, down for days and then the next time she put them on you could see it clicking through her head, what had happened last time and how she could make it better this time and that's how she seems to do it. She seems to go away and maybe not even think about it. (24)

We have almost no understanding of the processes that lead to this kind of learning though it appears that the brain, at an unconscious level, seems predisposed to search for patterns. Language learning offers one example, so do the ways in which different pieces of knowledge are related, in cryptic crossword clues for example. Many of us have had the experience of looking vainly at a clue only to find that a few hours later when we have moved on to totally different things, the solution springs at us as if from nowhere. Something must have happened in the brain meantime. This phenomenon has also been studied experimentally in relation to artificial grammars in which people can be shown to perceive patterns in visual displays though they are unaware of them at a conscious level (Reber, 1993). We are so imbued with the notion that learning must require deliberate effort that we tend to downplay what goes on subconsciously. A few parents had given more weight and some thought to the phenomenon.

> *Father*: I think that what happens is that they assimilate things which then disappear into somewhere that we are not conscious of and then it comes out as an emergent thing ... I think you get that, leaps and jumps forward with children anyway so that they can suddenly do something, probably applies to adults as well, but perhaps not to the same extent.
> *Mother*: Subconsciously they are absorbing and absorbing and absorbing, you don't see anything going on at all. It's like having a fallow period and then all of a sudden it comes up – like a seed sprouting under the soil. (15)

Observation

The pioneering work of Bandura (1977) established the role of observation in a social setting leads to imitation and the acquisition of social skills and attitudes. Parents were well acquainted with the ways in which children imitated observed behaviour in this way.

> They learn so much through watching the other kids, they watch and join in ... (24)

> [She] actually said once when she was looking after [the baby]. She looked really shy when I came in and said, 'I'm just giving him some mummy milk.' She's done that twice. Obviously it's a game and she's learned it through what she sees around. (25)

Far less recognized is the extent to which informal observation, and its auditory equivalent of listening, can lead to learning that is intellectual. This can occur implicitly by taking in information from the environment with little or no awareness; a level at which observation is barely removed from doing nothing. On the other hand it may refer to intent observation with the explicit aim of finding out about something and employing a tremendous amount of intellectual effort towards this end. Observation is the first learning strategy of the newborn child. The traditional belief that the world of the newborn infant is characterized by chaotic sensations of colour and noise has long been replaced following research which shows that neonates have well-developed cognitive structures which they use from birth to observe and begin to make sense of the physical and social world around them (e.g. Bremner, 1994; Schaffer, 1996; Smith, Cowie & Blades, 2003).

A great variety of knowledge, at a number of levels can be acquired through observation, as the following quotes help to illustrate. None of these refer to formal observation embedded in a structured lesson which is expected to lead to a given outcome. It is spontaneous and left to the child whether picked up implicitly or arising from curiosity or interest.

> Two summers ago, when she was ten, my daughter happened to join an adult discussion my in-laws were having on Parkinson's disease. She had watched a documentary, and used the information to explain that researchers are exploring brain injury as a possible cause of Parkinson's. Needless to say, the adults were slack-jawed in amazement. My daughter was oblivious. (8)

> She just knows things that you wouldn't imagine she could know. Sometimes she can tell you where she gets things from, sometimes she just knows them … she picks up from everybody, I think they all do. Watching them they are like little sponges and taking what they want, not what they have been told to take. (24)

> At this point, [the two boys, aged eleven and nine] neither of them read, or sort of … [but] there's a lot of learning gone on and a lot of information already collected in their computer of a brain. Some of that I have no idea where it came from, certainly not from conversing with me. Some of it I don't know. Sometimes I say really, how did you find that out? And sometimes they don't know where they found it out. They've heard it or … (2)

> There's something else with [her] that I've always noticed as well that you could maybe go somewhere and there's lots of things to take in and she just doesn't seem interested but she's obviously looking around, a few days later she's assimilated it all in her head, she's not talked about it, she's just obviously thought about it and then comes out with her own conclusion of what happened or theories. (24)

> The classic thing which would happen, I don't know at what age, it is when they are giving you back something that you know you haven't put in to that little head. It hadn't been said in that way or you didn't know your children were aware of this thing and suddenly it's coming out. (4)

While it may be acknowledged that observational learning that is implicit might lead to some low-level learning it is otherwise downplayed in our culture where the overriding emphasis is on instruction and explanation as the source of learning. Other cultures, however, place a great deal of reliance on informal observational learning which goes far beyond the social. Nicolaisen (1988) based on her research amongst the Punan Bah of the Borneo rain forest cites the importance of observation in a society where children are offered very little direct guidance by adults and in which questions are not encouraged. She describes learning as consisting largely of adult demonstration and child observation. Explanation or instruction is rare and children 'must use their eyes, and ears and reason a great deal on their own'. Any form of interaction between adults and children is seen as limited, nevertheless she is impressed by the children's 'amazing gift of participation' after having simply observed adult activities (p. 206). Through observation the Punan Bah children learn proper behaviour and a basic knowledge of social relationships and the ideational rationale behind them. As they get older they also learn work skills. Boys in particular she describes as learning by watching the men at work, for instance while they are making their fishing nets, although they make no contribution themselves until they are about nine or ten.

Following her research with Mexican children, Rogoff (2003) coins the phrase 'intent participation' to describe purposeful, observation-based learning. She suggests that where children mix with adults in their day-to-day activities and as they get on with their domestic, social and working lives the need for instruction or any manner of direct teaching is greatly reduced. She argues that simply through watching, children are able to pick up many of the skills and behaviours that they see around them. She illustrates her argument with examples taken from different cultures including Guatemala (citing, Nash, 1967) and Navajos (citing Collier, 1988). In both these examples she describes novice adults and children learning to weave simply through observing an adult weaver. The children who learned in this way were able to notice and infer from what was happening around them rather than relying on explanations of what the weaver was doing.

Our parents provided some examples of purposeful observation.

> [example of going for a walk at different times of the year] But you are also honing your observation skills as well because you know they are going to be different you are looking for differences. If I go for a walk and then do the same walk two days later I see the differences and she [daughter] understands as well that it changes all the time. (24)

> She's been on insect hunts and she spends a lot of time just finding them and watching them and sometimes she'll ask a question about them. (20)

> He takes something, 2D, a flat image and makes it into a 3D construction. It can look quite different in a diagram than it does when you put it together. But we just got him a big airball tower. It's a kind of series of tubes and bits that can bounce off – it's an air pressure system that pushes balls up a tube

and then they go boing, boing, boing, all over the place. And they were all shooting out a lot of the time when he first put it together. They wouldn't go round properly. He had to adjust all that to make sure that they hit the things that they were meant to hit. To see why they weren't hitting them and what he needed to do to make it work properly. He's actually very good at that. He's very good at visualizing that sort of thing in his head and then putting it together in 3D. (6)

An area in which intense observation appeared frequently in this study was drawing. This is an activity that children are actively encouraged to do in our society and also one that relies quite heavily on observation as well as imagination. Many children seemed to enjoy art as a way of exploring ideas and the things that they had seen.

[He] is very keen on birds, drawing birds, watching birds … (19)

One of the first ways she'd do it [explore an interest] is through art. She goes off to her table and pulls loads of stuff out and produces something off her own back. (25)

[He] has never been interested in writing things down, he'd much rather express it through drawing. (18)

[She] does it a lot through art [working things out], like trying to draw houses, the idea of a house, she'll do it over a few months. (25)

She is constantly sketching details and trying to get them right and getting quite annoyed if she can't get them right. (21)

Even where observation is utilized, in school science lessons for example, it is nearly always linked to verbal instruction and explanation. Rogoff (*et al.*, 2003) suggests that because children are so used to explanation-based methods of learning they may have lost the ability to learn through observation. She describes the difficulties encountered by her own daughter who wanted to have an Inuit game explained to her rather than learn by watching the other children. On the other hand, children educated informally, and who are in control of their learning, may make much more use of observation.

Conversation

Children like to talk. A teacher acquaintance of ours related to us an incident in her nursery class in which she was called out of the classroom for a few minutes and a teacher used to teaching at the upper end of the primary school took over.

After introducing himself and in keeping with good classroom management, he instructed the children that if anyone wanted to talk to him they had to put their hand up first. They all put their hands up. At this moment the class teacher returned to find her colleague a little perplexed. He told her he thought the children might be trying to wind him up as they had all put up their hands at the same time. 'Not at all' she replied. 'They like you. They all want to talk to you!' In school it is out of the question for children to engage in anything more than a fleeting conversation with their teacher. These children had not been in school long enough to know the meaning of the instruction in the school culture.

Of all the processes we discuss in this chapter, conversation is probably the one most frequently cited by parents. The role of at-home, social conversation between parents and children has been highlighted through the groundbreaking work of Tizard and Hughes (1984) who recorded and compared the conversations that young children of 3 and 4 had with their parents at home with those that they had with staff members in the school nursery class they attended on a half-time basis. The superior nature of the home conversations was revealed in both the quality of the language used and the intellectual content irrespective of parental background. Little is known about how far conversation might continue to offer the same benefits after reaching school age though it featured prominently in Alan's earlier research (Thomas, 1994, 1998). Here we explore the contribution of conversation to informal learning in greater depth.

We are not dealing here with the kind of directed dialogue between teacher and students in which the content is almost wholly aimed at what is being taught, itself the result of careful curriculum and lesson planning. Conversation at home is a social and therefore interactive process that can go in any direction, from everyday practical concerns to highly focused and intellectual discussion. Parents whose approach is informal certainly think it highly significant for learning.

> I actually think that conversational learning is the most significant element of their learning. In fact I'd probably go so far as to say that it probably accounts for 50% – equal to all the other methodologies put together. That would be my estimate in retrospect. (6)

> Conversation is a big thing, I was thinking about it this morning. What I do to a large extent is have long conversations with the children about things. (15)

> I think that a lot of their learning, a big percentage is through conversation, general knowledge I suppose ... [we talk about] anything, absolutely anything – could be the state of the environment to what we're going to cook for supper. (21)

Purposeful conversation is where a lot of learning takes place ... I am always looking to take it on a little bit further. (19)

We know a lot of adults, parents of their home education friends, so they can chat to them as well as to their friends of all different ages. And I suppose you learn things from other people don't you? They have surprising interests. (20)

It's interesting, the vivid memories, but one I have is taking [my partner] to an early bus because we have always taken him to work ... So when the kids were little I would have spent a lot of time in the car. I remember one morning at 7.30 or 8 o'clock, on the way home from dropping [him] off, the radio was on and there was some mention of Muslims and [she] launched a question from the back of the car. So I turned off the radio and we had a discussion and by the time we'd come home we'd covered all the world religions. I don't know, she was somewhere between four and seven and I remember stunning myself thinking God! She could be actually in school still getting through assembly but we've done this, like major ... Or it may be something like [when I exclaim] 'Oh my God!' when I hear something on the news and they'll ask me why did you react like that? And then I've got to explain myself. (4)

In family conversation, participants are of equal status, there is no controlling party or agenda and this is demonstrated in the twists and turns that a conversation might take.

I just think it's a natural process, that conversation takes place in a relaxed and natural environment rather than one in which there is a specific goal with an outcome, that by the end of this session you will know 'x'. Conversation just rambles around. It's non-threatening. There is no preconceived purpose but it's not purposeless. Natural conversation is not like a 'guided conversation' in school where the teacher is trying to 'draw out' certain points or answers. Real conversation always has a purpose but not an imposed one. A conversation at home might start with a question about B group vitamins from a cereal box and somehow the conversation covers fifteen different topics and ends up with the Chinese population problem and we're never sure of exactly how we got there. I think children learn very easily when they are interested in something and conversation enables us to wander through many topics. Sometimes they choose to follow something up, sometimes they just absorb things into their general knowledge and sometimes they lose interest and the conversation dies out. (5)

Parents naturally might try to extend the conversation but children did not feel constrained to listen. From the outside, this might seem like a lost opportunity; but it may be that children are selecting for themselves the optimum level or amount of knowledge they can take in at a given time.

> As soon as they think that you are trying to teach them something they tell you to shut up ... we find that we have to be really brief and to the point, just so that they get their questions answered really. ... They usually say, 'Mum you've gone on too long.' (21)

> I think to be honest with your children [you want] to give them as much information as possible with the result that they don't assimilate it – which I find a bit strange, the opposite to what I expected. ... They may find them [parent and child conversations] very boring a lot of the time unfortunately. (15)

> They have very good crap detectors like they can tell this is a lesson coming from Dad about something Dad believes with a certain amount of commitment or passion and it's coming from him and they can take it or leave it. And they do that all the time. So they will tell me to give over. (4)

On the other hand when it was of interest, conversation offered a multitude of learning possibilities with children as likely to generate a topic as their parents. First and perhaps most obviously, it is a way of transmitting information between people. Parents naturally pass a great deal on to their children – they know more about most things – but conversation is not about simply dumping information onto children. It's not one-to-one teaching. The following, rather longer extract, illustrates the interactive nature of conversation with participants dipping in and out, and playing an active part in moving the conversation on and around to address new areas or new angles.

> *Mother*: We might just be driving somewhere and a topic of conversation just comes up. It might be something they've been thinking about and then they start to talk about it and we all kind of join in with our different viewpoints. It gets expanded upon. It might be a factual thing like this thing about how does a nuclear bomb work? It might be more something to do with moral issues about how people treat other people. It might be something emotional that's affecting one of them at this time and they want to talk more about it. Anything, worries, stresses ...
> *Father*: Conversation happens a lot in the car. The car is one of the places where it's a kind of general down time. We're travelling and the reason I think that has played an important part in both our particular cases is that we are both pretty busy people. We tend to be doing lots of things which the children are welcome to join in or not join in. But in this time of

the car, we are travelling in and out of Limerick which we do quite a few times a week. We could listen to the radio which we sometimes do and we sometimes play a game but what mostly happens is that we converse. And it's not like anybody can wander off. We're all in the car together.

Mother: They might not listen if it's not interesting to them.

Father: They mostly do because they change the conversation if it's not interesting to them, just take it somewhere else. Quite a lot of those conversations where [two of us] are having a conversation and everybody else in the car is actually listening. So even when we are not participating actively we are participating passively and then an interjection might come in. In the short term it doesn't seem like it's much time. In retrospect, looking back at it, it's actually a considerable amount of very high quality time that just occurs ... It's one of those places where there are no distractions we haven't all seen many, many times before because we've been driving the route for ten years. And I think the constant little stimulus which isn't from us, it's from them. I might as well just say what's in the top of my head because we are sitting in the car and it's another twenty minutes before we get to Limerick and so anything and each of those little bits end up being very considerable because there's no pressure to drive the information out. I think one of the problems with a classroom type structure is, say, I do geography, I have this piece of information come in – it's quite stimulating and then I immediately go and do something quite different for another 40 minutes and that stuff that was in there was equally interesting or equally boring or whatever, gets pushed out by something else. Whereas here, because they choose the topics of conversation it tends to be grown on something they are naturally interested in and so it doesn't immediately get displaced by something of equal interest that's also being pushed in.

Daughter [aged 13]: Sometimes we'll be driving home in the car and I'll ask Dad a question like: How exactly does a nuclear bomb detonate or something? Then you get into this half-an-hour conversation about what exactly is the function of this, that and the other. What chemical changes go on? How exactly does the bomb destroy something? One thing leads to another.

Mother: A genteel example ...

Of course parents do not always have the information that their children might ask for or be able to offer the kind of input they would like. However, seeing another person challenged and observing how they consider a topic outside their area of knowledge may be a demonstration of thinking from which children can benefit. It is also of course an opportunity for parents to admit their ignorance. The upshot might be a genuine line of inquiry that both may share.

[I demonstrated] happiness to be ignorant about some things, which I think is one of the things which strikes me as really interesting about home education. Teachers often, I think, need to pretend that they know everything about something whereas if your child is interested in something and it is an area which you don't know about then you just say, 'I don't know, let's look it up' and I think that models the fact that you can find out about things that you don't know about ... So I think [I modelled] that inquisitive behaviour. (26)

Some parents considered the other side to conversation, in which parents listened rather than talked. Having someone to bounce ideas off or to think aloud to, can be very useful in straightening out thoughts about a subject or following through a difficult idea. Parents had both the time and inclination to be sympathetic listeners, no matter what the issue, offering a background against which the child could work out their own way forward.

She needs someone as a backboard, so even if I don't seem as if I'm interested, I would be, but she's using me as a backboard, bouncing off. (24)

I'd give her time and want to listen to her. (16)

For children listening can also be a very important way of picking up information and borders on observation. It is possible to be passively involved in a conversation and home-educated children probably have more chance than most to listen in to adult conversations. These may be casual or social conversations or equally more formal ones as when children accompany their parents to shops, banks, solicitors' offices, take family members to the doctor's, pets to the vets and the many other occasions when parents have to speak to outside agencies in a formal capacity. Incidentally, home educated children are far more likely to experience opportunities for learning in this way because they cannot be left at home unless there is someone there to look after them. From these conversations may be gleaned all manner of information on particular subject matters as well as on how society works and how adult relationships are ordered within society.

Exploration

Exploration covers a whole repertoire of techniques including thinking at varying levels, from simple, everyday questions, to investigating and researching a topic in depth.

Questions, questions, questions

Questioning is one of the most obvious manifestations of exploration. At home children can ask all the questions they want. It is a commonplace that most young children go through a phase of continuous questioning as they observe, pick up or think about things that arouse their curiosity. Tizard and Hughes (p. 102) discuss a young child's 'thirst for understanding' which they see as being pursued at first through physical exploration and later, as language develops, through verbal explorations. From this, they go on to develop their concept of intellectual search which they describe as being a conversation in which the child is 'actively seeking new information or explanations, or puzzling over something she does not understand, or trying to make sense of an apparent anomaly in her limited knowledge of the world' (p. 114). There has been very little in the way of follow up or extension of Tizard and Hughes' research with older children. This may be because in older children, formal education allows little opportunity for, or attaches little value to, the things which children explore for themselves though there may be a lot of rhetorical support for it. Among home-educated children, however, we found that the concept of intellectual search could be expanded for these older children to include not only the mostly short conversational exchanges recorded by Tizard and Hughes but also much longer sustained inquiries.

For many of the home-educated children their questioning phase continued far beyond the age traditionally associated with it. Parents saw this kind of self-initiated inquiry as of overwhelming educational importance, although coping with it was not always easy.

> The key thing with autonomy is that you must be there to answer questions. (19)

> It is an integral part of the whole process that they ask you things that they are concerned about and that they want to know. That's almost the bedrock of our approach to education, that it stems from their interest. (15)

> Sometimes I can't hear another question. Sometimes the questions are incessant. I don't mean 'can we?' questions. I mean 'What?' and 'Why?' questions. And it starts when they are two or three doesn't it. Then by the time they go to school it seems to drop. When they are in school they can't have many questions answered and when they get home they don't feel like asking questions any more … If I decide I'm going to do something with them like I did this morning, I never get further than the initial introduction because of the number of questions they ask. It goes wider and you can even change from one subject to another. (9)

One day I said to [him] do not ask me one more question. I cannot cope with one more question. He looked at me and said: 'but I have to. It's my job'. (2)

A lot of home education learning is through questions. There is generally time to answer them. Sometimes the questions can be quite exhausting though. I don't mind not knowing the answers. I just say, 'I don't know.' Sometimes we'll look it up in the encyclopaedia. Or it might be in this book or we can have a look in the library, go on the internet or sometimes it's a matter of 'I haven't got time right now ...' The exhausting bit is when the questions just don't stop and I might be tired or under pressure trying to get something else done and I just feel bombarded. However the children do become more independent with finding answers themselves as they get older. The eldest [aged 14] habitually uses the dictionary. He and his brother [aged 11] know how to look things up in the encyclopaedia, books or on the internet. [The 9 year old] knows that's what you do to find the answer to questions but he doesn't do it independently yet. (5)

Wondering and working out

Sometimes wanting to know something is not so straightforward. Perhaps there is no one to ask, perhaps you are not meant to know, perhaps the speculation is more interesting than the answer. The things that can interest children (and maybe adults) the most are not always facts that can be looked up in books. They are things about the world and the people and the interaction and ideas that make up life immediate to them. The following incident describes such a piece of curiosity and the intellectual busyness which it generated.

Natalie, Pippi and Henry began to puzzle over the relationship between one of the coaches and one of the children at their Saturday soccer club. They had picked up from the way that these two interacted with each other that there was more to their relationship than coach and club member and now they wanted to know what. A number of speculative conversations, taking place over a period of weeks, considered the various possibilities. Hypotheses were made, considered, elaborated and, either dismissed or retained to be tested against further evidence when it became available. One interesting point which emerged from watching their speculation was the extent to which children are still working out situations which are immediately clear to adults. This is a point made by Tizard and Hughes (1984) and a factor which increases the amount of intellectual effort which children, as compared to adults, must put into the finding out process. The coach they knew, from information gleaned through eavesdropping, to be 16 or 17 years old. However they still wondered, and had to assess the possibility, that a child of their own age might be his son. Of course, after due consideration they were able to dismiss this possibility.

It soon became crucial to gather some move evidence in order to move their investigation forward. Again they discussed at length; what would be the most important thing to know and what would be the best way to go about finding it out. In the end already knowing the coach's surname Henry was tasked with asking the younger boy what his first name was. It was felt that he could pose this question most successfully because he was the youngest and young children do ask odd things. Their handling of this part of the problem demonstrated an astute awareness of their own status as children. They could use this status and the different ways in which children are treated to their advantage; i.e. by asking a question which they knew would be regarded as intrusive from an adult but acceptable from a child. Even so they appointed the youngest candidate to perform the task, showing their awareness of the social niceties of the situation. It turned out to be a good question, revealing that the two did share a surname, although it did not explain the exact relationship. A little while later, the coach signed a soccer school certificate using a different surname and the debate opened up again. This time the children constructed a family scenario which involved divorce and remarriage and which might be able to account for both the use of two surnames and the relationship between the two.

Throughout this investigation the children were driven by sheer nosiness; the facts of the relationship would have no meaning to them; they were not even particular friends of the boy concerned. The point is, however, that for the children it was a very interesting subject and one in which they invested a good deal of speculative thought, building hypotheses, coming up with ways to test their ideas, assessing and re-assessing their evidence and eventually drawing conclusions. Not only this, they also had to draw on other areas of knowledge; their understandings of divorce and the social circumstances around it; how a remarriage might lead to a change of surname and some unusual relationships. The triviality of the subject matter went a long way towards masking the rigorous mental activity that went into pursuing this subject. Where the adults were aware of it, the inquiry was treated as something of a running joke; very differently to the way in which they would have considered questions about life in a Medieval town or how an electric motor works. For the children though it was every bit as serious, if not more so. (14).

Self-directed learning

Other forms of self-directed learning were described by parents as they watched their children become involved in different pastimes. One parent saw small children playing and experimenting as the early basis of scientific inquiry.

You see, I guess to put into words from an educational perspective, they were learning scientific method. They were learning how to experiment with different media with sand and water, with playdough, with paint: if I put my hand in the paint and put it on the wall it gets transferred to the wall and I think I need to repeat that experiment several hundred times to make sure that it happens every time. And then they know something about print. They know that it sticks on stuff and that it transfers to other stuff. As a parent of young children you take that for granted. That's just what kids do and if you are not thinking about it as being learning, as being a scientific process, people don't put value on it and 'oh they are mucking around with water, they are mucking around with bubbles'. But you watch what they do. It's very scientific what they do in terms of making a hypothesis and testing a hypothesis and then adjusting their hypothesis depending on the results of their test. Repeatability is very important to young kids because the world is very chaotic to young children and unpredictable and they love it when they've worked something out and they know what's going to happen and they can predict the handprint's going to come out bright red on the wall. And it happens again and again and every time they predict it, it comes true. (3)

Others also referred to experimenting in older children:

Most of hers is not book learning, mostly trying things out, experimenting. (16)

They have learned things like the paint programme almost entirely through trial and error and experimenting on their own. (14)

With [him] his curiosity manifests itself in that he tries to break things ... to take things apart, see how they work. (15)

Research sources include books, the internet and seeking outside expertise.

The older ones do more reading or research. Research in [his] case in that he always spends a lot of the day researching information about computer games. ... I suppose we used the internet and we got a lot of books and we met local people and made friends in the village ... [in order to find out more about the subject] it was a case of seeing what worked and what didn't work. (20)

When extended into a project or other undertaking this latter kind of learning may appear nearer to what children in school do when they are required to research a given topic, road accidents or life in Roman times for example. In informal learning however, it is children who choose whether or not to follow up an interest. They will also decide how to pursue the topic, how far to pursue it and whether or not to write or record anything. They can take or leave any suggestions from their parents. They may also go off on any tangent that captures their interest. At home, this choice and control over what to learn serves as a powerful motivator that can lead to considerable, sometimes adult-level skill or knowledge of a chosen topic. Examples we came across, in some cases taken well beyond what might be expected for children of their age, included: Japanese culture, piano, guitar, cello, novel writing, military history, weaving, computing, welding, bee-keeping, football strategy and tactics, electronics, rabbitting, ballistics, aircraft and boat design, metalwork, alternative energy. It would obviously be difficult to pursue most of these without some expert guidance which the children obtained from a variety of sources, within the family and outside. Of course there is no special virtue in becoming highly specialized. Many children had a wide range of interests, as we have seen, which they followed for as long as the interest held.

The following is an example of a sustained hobby pursued, without any external guidance, over what turned out to be years. Once again, alongside the specific subject knowledge gained, intellectual skills, including those of researching, experimenting, problem solving and reverse engineering, have been practised, tested and honed and could be used to tackle virtually any other given subject matter.

Beading by Natalie

> We got into beading when Pippi made a chunky necklace for a birthday gift. I had a look in the bead box and found some seed beads and decided to have a go with them, our hobby has just grown from there. We experimented and learned how to do flowers, blocks, loops, fringes and tassels. Lots of things we learned to do by accident! We bought an Egyptian beading set and tried a new kind of beading with wire, which we had not done before except for making wire animals. Then we dug out an African bead set we had a long time but never used; from that we learned how to do peyote stitch. Beading's a challenge and sometimes very frustrating, but great fun and well worth the effort. Beading is never boring, there's always loads of new things to try! (Written by Natalie)

Natalie's parents made the following observations on their daughter's hobby.

> From the simplest of beginnings, beading and jewellery making in general has grown into a full blown hobby in which Natalie (aged 10 when she began) has learned a variety of techniques and produced jewellery good enough to not only sell at fund-raising events but also to attract orders from some customers.

Incidentally to learning to make jewellery, Natalie has learned snippets about beading in other cultures and times, the social and cultural significances of jewellery, design, symmetry and patterns. She has kept an order book, made her own advertising material, purchased her own materials, priced her finished products, run her own stall at a home-educating event and assisted with sales at other fund-raising events. However, even this practical experience is just the tip of the learning iceberg as far as her hobby is concerned. Intellectually jewellery making has demanded an eclectic approach: experimenting, reading up, following instructions, attending a workshop, reverse engineering, trial and error, analysing mistakes, capitalizing on some happy accidents, working from her own visualization. Working alone, no pre set route to improvement was available, she had to decide for herself what to try next by advancing her own ideas or seeking inspiration elsewhere. Part of the pleasure of a hobby is this challenge in moving forward, trying out and achieving new things. She has picked her own projects, set her own goals and overcome her own difficulties. It has also involved frustration, set backs, the need to amend ideas and even on occasions to make the decision to give up on an idea or a project that is just not working out. Considerable mental energy has been directed into both the use of external resources and the pursuance of her own self-generated ideas. (14)

Practice

Practice lies in a slightly different category to the other activities discussed here. Practice is the repetition of something already learned.

Children spontaneously learn through practice almost from birth. Apart from practising basic sensorimotor skills, babies spontaneously babble, gradually approximating and repeating speech sounds of the language they hear around them. When they start talking they practise their words. Sometimes this practice appears to be undertaken for its own sake rather than as an attempt to communicate for example practising words, alone in bed at night.

Practice, usually seen as a mainstay of formal education, is equally significant in consolidating and improving skills and confidence in informal learning. It is the way that practice takes place in informal learning that differs. Children decide for themselves when, what and how to practise and how much practice is necessary for their purpose.

> It's practice from a self-motivated point of view. Rather than having a teacher say, 'You need to practise these to develop automatic response' or something like that, it is the child thinking, 'I want to be able to write like Mum and Dad so ...' and then they practise. (5)

A lot of informal practice may also be embedded in a real-life context so that it is not immediately obvious, even to the learner, that any practice is taking place. It also differs in another way from practice in the classroom because it can be more a question of trying out, taking a step towards full understanding experimenting, as well as consolidating knowledge.

> I do remember them counting up to as far as they could count up to because they wanted to see how far they could count. And lying in bed and [one of them] saying: Hey! I've got up to a hundred. And then saying ok and both saying ok, let's see if we can get any further. This was when they were four or five and seeing how far they could get. (1)

> *Child 1*: You have to put it in here. You are not at liberty to do as you please.
> *Child 2*: What does liberty mean?
> *Child 1*: I don't know. (14)

Children also like repetition though not in the sense of doing an exercise. The enjoyment of this, with its opportunity to practise, can be seen in the way that young children show great enthusiasm for hearing the same story over and over again. When they start to read, it seems that, given the opportunity, they like to re-read favourite books, sometimes several times over. In her longitudinal study of literacy, Bissex (1980) describes her son gaining fluency and expressiveness in doing so, pointing out that this sort of enthusiastic practice through re-reading was not provided for in his school reading schemes.

The following neatly captures the difference between voluntary and imposed practice.

> It seems to be what children become passionate about, practising what they want to learn. [One of my sons] is probably my best example of that. Since the day he was able to open his mouth he sang all day every day other than asking questions. That's been his life. The minute he could play the piano … I taught him little bits of that and [his older brother] encouraged him as well … He was out busking at the age of five on drums with [his brothers]. He'd learned a little bit about several instruments. At one point, for six months he would play the piano for at least an hour. He'd play the guitar and the drums for an hour. We might have lunch and he'd go back and do the whole thing over again and daily for six months he'd just play instruments over and over and over again.
>
> I'd been brought up in a family where my mother wanted us to learn piano. I was passionate about singing and dancing but my mother wanted us to learn piano. I learnt piano for eight years and it was a nightmare. We had to do this amount of practice. In my early years I loved it because the piano was in my grandmother's house. She would sit with me and I would

play and we would chat. I really enjoyed that but that was viewed as not serious enough. So the piano was taken to our home where we had to sit and do an hour's practice. I hated that. I'd learnt the skill of being able to read [a book] and play the piano at the same time because it was way too boring. I didn't want to reproduce that with my children. What came out of that for me was an inability to enjoy piano. I thought what's the point of knowing how to play something if you are not going to enjoy it. (2)

Summing up

The activities we have discussed in terms of their contribution to informal learning in this chapter derive largely from parental observations and reflections. Within these we can see how implicit, incidental and self-directed learning all have a part to play. There is a danger however, that by concentrating on how children might acquire academic knowledge informally we have not emphasized enough that these children do not see themselves as learners. They simply get on with life, doing the things which appeal to them and through these things learning is stimulated, whether that takes the form of finding out about an intriguing step-relationship or something more 'academic'. From the child's point of view they are simply involving themselves in their environment; it is adults who chose to impose such categories as 'intellectual', 'academic' or 'useful'. Through their involvement, learning expands along twin trajectories; the acquisition of new information alongside the honing of all manner of thinking and research skills. Children are learning how to find out and practising how to learn without this being in any way imposed on them.

Chapter 6

Parents

In the preceding two chapters we concentrated on the subject matter and processes of informal learning. The part played by parents, although crucial and manifesting itself in a variety of ways, has not been the focus of our attention. The main purpose in this short chapter is to identify the chief ways in which parents facilitate learning.

Parents have an important part to play in education regardless of whether or not their children are in school. It has been known since the pioneering research of Douglas (1967) that home background is critical to educational achievement in school. In a recent and wide-ranging review of research concerned with the impact of parental involvement, parental support and family education on the achievement of pupils in school Desforges and Abouchaar (2003) found unanimous agreement for the proposition that much of what underlies achievement in school is to be found in children's home lives. This is so even though parents may only be with their children for a short time each day. Their review consistently shows that 'good parenting' is uniquely influential on children's achievement even when all other factors, such as socio-economic status, are taken out of the equation. The parental involvement that they talk about can take many forms but generally includes 'provision of a secure and stable environment, intellectual stimulation, parent-child discussion, good models of constructive social and educational values and high aspirations relating to personal fulfilment and good citizenship' (p. 4).

By the nature of the task which they have undertaken home-educating families are almost guaranteed to fulfil the greater part of Desforges and Abouchaar's 'good parenting' ideals. In fact the interviews showed parents providing these factors in abundance. In this sense, what home-educating parents do with their children is not so much a radical departure but simply an extension of what is considered to be good parenting anyway. However, whilst Desforges and Abouchaar obviously expect schools to build on this base, in the home-educating families very little, if any, further pedagogical role was taken up by parents. Remarkably it seems that parenting, rather than teaching, is sufficient to enable children to learn.

From the preceding two chapters we have drawn together and categorized what parents do to facilitate learning. They act as role models; they share their own knowledge; they mediate access to the culture in a variety of ways; they act as co-learners; they hold aspirations for and expectations of their children. In day-to-day terms these are, of course, not delineated categories of parental behaviour but are very much part and parcel of the parental role as promoted by our society. They are practised by the large majority of parents of pre-school children and continue as a natural matter of course for older children educated informally at home.

Parents as role models

Parents are role models by virtue simply of going about their own business in the proximity of their children. They model the use of certain skills and certain behaviours without any intention to teach or even any expectation that their children will learn, but simply as part of their own lives. They discuss things with partners and other adults on all manner of issues from the intellectual to the trivial and from world affairs to family matters. At a practical level they undertake a wide range of everyday tasks such as cooking, cleaning, child care, shopping, gardening and finance. The home educating way of life, in which children spend much more time with adults as they conduct their everyday domestic lives, creates the conditions of 'spontaneous apprenticeship' (Miller, quoted in Smith, 1988, p. 64) in which children learn from adults by watching, helping, imitating and, if they need to, asking questions.

This parent made explicit reference to the idea of both an apprenticeship and the way in which parents were role models for their children.

> For the skills that he has picked up and virtually taught himself and he's had people around that he can ask questions of, friends that have got skills, really like an informal apprenticeship. Maybe that is a good way of pointing out to people how autonomous learning works, you can say it's like an apprenticeship in life, isn't it? You are just watching how everyone else does things and asking them questions when you need to. (22)

Another parent saw her own attitude towards learning as providing a model for her children to emulate:

> I modelled for them caring behaviour, interest in things, happiness to be ignorant about some things which I think is one of the things which strikes me as really interesting about home education is teachers often, I think, need to pretend that they know everything about something whereas if

> your child is interested in something and it is an area which you don't know about then you just say, 'I don't know, let's look it up' and I think that models the fact that you can find out about things that you don't know about. (26)

Some parents extended on the idea of an apprenticeship in life by pointing out how they expected children to make some practical contribution within the family. Both the motivation and the style of this learning finds echoes in the lives of children in other cultures where parents' chief motivation may be to extract reliable and real contributions from their children as soon as they can, rather than seeing childhood as a protracted learning period during which most children have no practical role (Gaskins, 1999; Guberman, 1999).

> I am very interested, I am motivated in my children learning well because I am expecting them to do the things to lighten my load. I require them as they get older to take on more functions at home, to cook, to clean, washing, read to the younger ones, do things for themselves that I have had to do up until then. (16)

Mediators

Parents mediate both learning processes and the informal curriculum itself. They do this by providing the circumstances and tools by which children can, for themselves, explore the informal curriculum. In practical terms this means taking them out and introducing them to the world and providing the wherewithal for them to engage with the artefacts of their culture: toys and books, pencils, paper, TVs, computers, money, household equipment, kitchens to cook in, gardens to grow things in and so on. These that are important in the culture and which the culture uses to understand and disseminate knowledge allows children to engage further themselves with the cultural curriculum. Once again this is very normal behaviour for all parents in our society; the only difference being that home-educating parents do much more of it.

Children find access to the informal curriculum outside the home, not just through deliberate induction but as their parents go about their own business and get on with their own lives. Parents go to shops, banks, the doctor's, church, the hospital, solicitors' offices. They catch buses, park the car, cross roads, pay for things, read signs, hurry to be on time and so on. We have already pointed out how much children may pick up about the world around them from these types of trips – snippets on how society works, literacy, numeracy, geography, the importance of time and money and so on. In addition, all the parents we spoke to put effort into introducing their children to places, people and opportunities which they felt would be of interest and/or benefit to them. They join groups, libraries and clubs, go to museums and on outings, seek out sporting and social opportunities. In these ways parents are acting as mediators, providing their children access to new areas of the informal curriculum. Many parents, particularly of the older children, described themselves as facilitators. They acted to support or make possible their children's pursuance of their own interests by providing transport, finances, equipment and so on.

Passing on knowledge

Parents and children who spend a lot of time together interact with each other a great deal. They talk together, play together, work together, and through this interaction parents have innumerable opportunities to pass on their knowledge. Parents answer questions, pass comments, draw children's attention towards things that they are interested in or think their children might be, or communicate knowledge incidentally in the course of casual chat. This is very different from the sort of transmission that teaching in school aims at. Even the use of questioning is very different. Questions in school are a tool chiefly used by the teacher in order to establish how much children know. At home it is more likely to be the children who use questions to find out more about what interests them (e.g. those in Tizard and Hughes' study). (Some home-educating children, on starting school later on, are perplexed that it is the teachers who ask most of the questions when it is the students who are doing the learning!) The questioning techniques of teachers are much less likely to be needed at home because what a child does and does not know will emerge quite naturally during the course of conversation on the matter of interest. Parents can fill these gaps either deliberately, if this is appropriate, or simply by contributing to their child's thinking through their own comments or questions.

Parents also assist children with things they want to achieve, from getting dressed to writing an important letter. In line with neo-Vyotskian theories of instruction (discussed in Chapter 3), scaffolding is important but with one crucial difference. It is not the adult who, having decided what to teach, assesses the child's level of knowledge and then leads him on to the next level as determined by the child's developing understanding. For informal learners, while the metaphor of scaffolding might hold, the process is otherwise turned on its head. It is generally the child, not the teacher, who leads the process. Moreover the starting point is the child actually wanting the knowledge in question. Barbara Rogoff's research for example leads her to conclude that children actively 'seek, structure and even demand the assistance of those around them in learning how to solve problems of all kinds' (Rogoff, 1991: 68). It is a style of learning with which home-educating parents are very familiar.

Co-learning

As has been pointed out before, parents are not always themselves in the position to hand knowledge on. Children's diverse range of interests means that parents are often unable to fill the role of expert. In such cases parents and children frequently become co-learners. This was invariably viewed as a positive aspect of informal learning as well as being very much in contrast with school where the teacher is nearly always presumed to have prepared the topic in advance, even if it is subsequently 'explored' together with the class.

Learning as a joint venture provides opportunities for discussion, exploration, experimentation and brainstorming that probably would not exist where one party is already an expert. It also provides a symmetry in the learning relationships where the contributions of both parent and child are of equal value and importance in furthering the knowledge and understanding of both parties. This is likely to foster children's confidence in their own ability to learn and to help the development of thinking and communicating skills such as assessing ideas, mixing approaches, trying things out and meeting other people's thinking half way. With older children shared learning might simply mean being a sounding board in response to what their children were learning independently.

Of course a lot of parent-child interaction is not about learning or even passing on knowledge or finding out. It is simply about being together, doing things together and enjoying each other's company. Unlike school where learning is delivered in a purposeful manner and in set chunks of time as lessons, parent-child interaction at home is an ongoing aspect of life. Within this, learning may equally occur in a one word answer to a question or a long discussion returned to over days; it may be a passing suggestion made about a game or an in-depth investigation on a matter of mutual interest that could take place over years. Much might be of a very subtle nature, barely recognizable as it is sandwiched in to some joint activity with completely different aims.

Expectations

The four main areas of parental input which we have described above simply build on what most parents of young children do before they go to school. This type of taken-for-granted input is accompanied by an equally taken-for-granted expectation that children will respond to it. We have very deep-seated expectations that small children will be interested in certain things and that they will learn certain things. When children begin school parental expectations are necessarily tempered and affected by school performance. Children who are doing well may be expected to continue in the same vein, but parents whose children are not meeting school standards will be forced to adjust their own expectations. The home-educating parents were not subject to these constraints.

They were able to show confidence in their children regardless of their levels of achievement; many were not even particularly aware as to whether or not their children were meeting school standards. Even late reading was not viewed as any kind of barrier to future academic achievement (see Chapter 8). The expectation that their children would be able to create and fulfil their own ambitions was very high. As one parent said with regard to her son:

> [He] hasn't a clue what he wants to do but I don't think that that's a problem because he's certainly going to be capable of doing any number of things. It's not something I'm worried about. (21)

To sum up the kind of parental input we have been describing is very much that which is expected of 'good' parents in our society. It is offered as a matter of course to pre-school children and is clearly an important contributor to the great deal of cultural knowledge and skills which small children acquire before they begin school. School itself necessarily curtails such parental contributions. The expectation behind Desforges and Abouchaar's review is that parents are creating a background or adjunct to formal instruction. The home-educated children however have no equivalent in their lives to the teaching provided by school. For them this is no adjunct. *It is all there is.*

Chapter 7

Play as a vehicle for learning

When children learn informally and are able to choose how they spend their time, a great deal of it is devoted to play, certainly up to early adolescence. Parents stressed the importance of play to their children; how much they seemed to personally gain from it, as well as considering it a vehicle for learning. This is in stark contrast to the view held by those who would see older children being allowed to play all day as irresponsible parenting. The first part of the chapter describes how parents viewed play. The second part illustrates in great detail how play contributes to learning of an intellectual nature in two very different situations: learning to play football and a fantasy game. As well as illustrating informal learning processes these make the point that the kind of learning most valued in school, verbal reasoning, can be developed in what on the surface appear to be only recreational activities.

When children play they are very much in control. Any help sought is usually to meet the requirements of what is being played. There is widespread agreement on the contribution which play makes to children's development during the pre-school years. Through play, children demonstrate their self-perceived relationship to the cultural curriculum, acting out countless cultural scenarios, taking adult roles and dealing with adult and family behaviours, customs and dilemmas, including moral ones. In this way they identify themselves as members of their family, cultural and sub-cultural groupings. Play also provides a meaningful setting for the exploration of intellectual skills, such as literacy and numeracy. Hall (1994), for example, describes children spontaneously including written material and writing into their play.

As play matures through infancy to early childhood, so it may continue to rise to new levels of sophistication in later childhood. Whilst children continue to play when not in school, certainly into the early secondary years, teachers and parents generally see this as 'time out' rather than having any intellectual potential. Home educators on the other hand, perhaps because they are more likely to observe the intellectual processes involved in play, commonly remark, in newsletters and other personal accounts, on the large amount of time their children spend playing and on its educational value. Particularly visible are the exploratory aspects of play; the questions and intellectual searches which arise while playing. Not only are the issues raised demanding ones, but finding solutions to them is treated as an important matter by the children concerned. In addition to this, play demands its own logical structure; things in games do not happen at random, even a fantasy game is set within certain parameters. In the sophisticated games of older children, casual observation reveals not just the unfolding of a storyline, but the unfolding of imaginary characters and the reactions of these characters to each other and to events. Thus the game, like a well-written novel, is following action through on a number of simultaneously occurring planes. Cohen and MacKeith (1991) in their detailing of children's imaginary worlds reveal some of the amazingly intellectual demands which children can make of themselves when apparently just playing. They are particularly concerned with children's creations of their own fantasy worlds, although much of what they describe is also to be found in more casual and shorter-lived play episodes. Sometimes these fantasy worlds grow into many-faceted, absorbing hobbies and entail highly sophisticated thinking and activities which would far more usually be described as work than play. Examples include the creation of languages, secret scripts, railway timetables, maps, documents, histories, written and spoken stories and traffic flow management to name but some. The creative, imaginative and resourceful thinking and learning which such playing demands seems theoretically limitless.

Play appeared so widespread, to cover so many activities and to take up so much time that getting a grip on its essential elements was tricky for parents, but they clearly saw it as a very important part of their children's lives. This parent, like others, returned to play again and again throughout the interview

What is playing? It's life half the time. (24)

It sounds as if it's not hard work, play is something that sounds superfluous to life and yet our children do it 75% of their time. It's not frivolous, it's part of their life. (24)

Everything she does is a game, even if she's writing or whatever she's doing it's also a game. (24)

They just play a lot, all of our kids do. (24)

Others reiterated the same themes:

Mainly what they do is play with their friends. (15)
She likes to always be seeing what people are playing, they make up their own games all the time. (25)

It's very hard to distinguish between play and whatever the opposite is, probably work or doing nothing ... I would say that they are playing all the time, that has just never stopped. (21)

They would play with anything, they never ran out of inspiration, they had constant ideas about what to do, endless imagination in their games. (14)

And for the children themselves:

Child: We play, get washed and dressed, then play, then breakfast, then play. We just keep on playing. (14)

The sheer amount of time and effort that children put into playing means that its importance, at least to the children doing it, cannot be overlooked. When one of us spent most of the day with the family of the first parent quoted below the youngest child, aged six, spent the whole time outside the house playing on a pile of builders' sand with toy lorries, interrupted only by the need to eat.

I suppose he would recognizably play more than [his older sisters] because he plays with his toys all day long. He's got some CD Roms he uses quite a lot, particularly when he's got some friends around, like [one who] comes round – they both love Legoland and stuff ... They spend hours playing different games, digging the sandpit; they build roads and bridges and that kind of thing ... A lot of them have a kind of story attached to them. They are kind of saying the story as they are building and going along ... (6)

I think play comes from within them. It's not imposed on them. Although more and more we do impose play on our kids but true play comes from within. They are exercising their choice and they're in control in some ways. So they're building mastery over their world and they can control the parameters. When [he] builds a Lego train yard under his bed he can choose everything. He's only limited by the materials he's working with. And so I think that gives children a tremendous sense of power or ability or a sense of operating within the world. I'm sure it's not conscious, but it's having a positive influence on their surroundings. The openness of it and the lack of control that anyone exerts on them, that is also part of the equation. Often there's another family with home-school kids who come over every Wednesday afternoon. I don't ever plan what it is we are going to do, I don't even have to think about it – whether they choose a game or whether they get out a book of outdoor games and adapt a game to suit them, they are off and gone. I don't have to do anything. All I have to do is call them in for a snack and that's it. And I just think it's part of creating their own world, being themselves, who they are. (8)

Many parents referred directly to both the social and intellectual aspects of learning through play.

> We see it as playing but it's not, it's their education ... I think that they learn through play and I still do. (24)

> I suppose, if they are playing with other children, they are learning how to get on with other children. ... I suppose they learn how to resolve conflicts to some extent, hopefully, how to read other people's feelings. (15)

> There's language development ... and of course they are creating scenarios, if not stories and situations which do require solutions. (19)

Certainly play has the scope to extend in a variety of directions and to blend into other processes from straightforward flights of the imagination to narrative building, creative writing, role play in real-life scenarios, observation, questioning and logical sequencing.

> Another way my kids work things out is that if you present them with something or they get an idea from the TV they just act it out as a game then for a while. (25)

> I overhear them playing and using a phrase I've said to them maybe a month before. Especially the telling off thing I'm finding with [them] at the minute; punishment seems to be coming up in their games so they're learning that kind of thing, the ways of the world through it, 'If you do that, then I'm going to ...' It's through play that they try to come and understand the world. (25)

> They were acting out roles, sometimes one would be the boss or an authority type figure like teacher and child and they would act out those situations. (15)

> She makes up a lot of stories that she does not want to write down. She talks to herself a lot, in her own world, her own inventions and that can be for hours at a time ... it's playing and learning. (20)

> I notice that things they have learnt through conversation get acted out in play. Because my children love books and movies their games often end up being written up as books or movie scripts. In a sense their play becomes their plotting – they try out different scenarios and see what works and what doesn't. (5)

Play could be endlessly mind stretching:

> And it never works out the same twice because two children playing the same game will always want to do something slightly different so you have the same scenario five days in a row and they are playing a completely different game and I can see them getting completely different things from it. It's like taking a walk in the countryside, you go in spring and you see completely different things to when you go in autumn, to winter, to summer. (24)

> This flexibility in play, the endless possibilities for mixing in new experiences is what allows play to grow with the child and to keep on providing interest and challenge. One of their favourite games is to build a little town with their Playmobil and create characters who interact with each other and do different things. They have done this type of thing for years and have created real stories with characters and scenarios which have developed along sequential and logical lines of narrative. But very recently a whole new dimension has been added in that they have introduced a money economy. The main characters in the current game have jobs and earn money which they then have to spend in order to provide the income for the other players. Needless to say this has raised a whole host of problems and issues many of which are pertinent to real life basic economics. If you wanted to assess the game from an 'educational' viewpoint, they are actually studying economics: supply and demand, first- and second-class goods, pricing policies, the effects of saving and spending, unemployment etc. They even set up a tax system to help even out some of the income discrepancies that kept occurring. (14)

Some parents went even further and pointed out how play might push out into other realms, what adults in new situations do or even insights into other people's beliefs.

> After going to the pub again after a very long while and you see the younger people putting on this sort of persona, so even at that age, at 20 they're still acting out. Even as a parent you are still acting out different things. (25)

> He'd made this big mound of sand which took hours and he'd made holes in it and he'd made little pathways up to it and there were things growing out of it and he had this whole world going on in this sand. There wasn't a toy in sight, it was totally imagination and I said to him, 'think about what you are doing now and think about how say the Aztecs believed in the spirit of things and how they left offerings. Even now some cultures will leave offerings on graves because they believe that the spirits will

take them, you believe in your game that these little things, these little footprints, this is your game and your belief. This is how religion and beliefs grow out of conviction that this is what happens and this is what is happening in your game and this is no different to an Egyptian sending something off or a Viking putting things in a grave for use in the afterlife' and he had literally left little bits of twigs for these little characters to use. (18)

Home-educated children who have the time and the freedom to do so, may continue playing long past the age where formal pedagogy sees it as a useful activity.

And they still learn through playing. They all play with this castle with the little knights [in the corner of the room] And [while playing] with that they are learning through their interest in history. Even [the eldest] who is nearly 13 plays with that. I notice some of his friends who are older still play. Because they are with their siblings a lot there's not so much ageism. (9)

Or that imaginative energy may become the fuel for other activities, defined rather differently as adult creative pursuits.

[The children, aged 12 and 14] like making films and they have done since we've had a camera, whether it is animated or using whatever to making a film with a video camera, they've been doing that for years and it is definitely play, you couldn't say that it was work and that just goes on, they are always doing that ... it's kind of developed from fantasy to acting. (21)

[Talking about her son's computer game] It's a fantasy game; he's a character in the game that's total fantasy. (21)

[My daughter, aged 14] spends a lot of her spare time reading or writing. There's a list that she's joined called The Silver Mountain – it's a website on the subject of wolves and you have characters that you write about and you have to be extremely literate or the site does not accept your post, it has to be over a certain length and you are writing about your wolf's character. (20)

[Interviewer suggests to parent that child's interest in filming is an example of play]
Son (aged 14): It's not play! It's making movies!
Mother: His objection is that what he does is not play. It's serious work. [To her son] Ok. Your objection is noted and it will go down in the

transcript. From an adult's point of view it looks like play.
Son: But it isn't play!
Mother: Ok.
Son: Board games and computer games – they are play. (5)

Learning the rules of football through observation and reasoning

The following lengthier illustration, provided by family 14, shows some of the learning necessitated by taking up a new sport and how three children went about accomplishing this. Although sport is not usually considered an area in which intellectual skills are at the forefront, a detailed examination of how the children went about learning to play football shows that observation backed by considerable logical reasoning formed their main approach. As this example illustrates, the development of reasoning, along with techniques such as hypotheses building, testing and refining, can take place in settings which might easily be dismissed as of no intellectual significance. However, this type of observation and working out could form the approach to a number of subjects, and certainly many of those included in the school curriculum.

Henry was five, his sisters eight and ten when they joined a local children's football club. It was a new kind of experience for all three of them with obvious social and physical dimensions, but also intellectual aspects. Observation was the first strategy used on the learning curve as they got to grips with their new hobby.

Before joining the Saturday Soccer School the children's experience of football had involved no more than the casual kicking of a ball around the garden. They had never played or watched an organized game, not even on television and had never displayed any greater interest in football as either a sport or an aspect of culture. Both their parents were similarly football illiterates. Nevertheless when they saw a field full of small boys playing on a sunny Saturday morning, it looked fun and a way of getting to know some other children in a new area. Henry expressed an interest and so it was that he set off to join the football club. An entry from his mother's diary describes the magnitude of the learning task as encountered at his first session:

> The first thing that became immediately and forcefully obvious, at least to me on the side lines, was how little about football any of us knew, but that even I knew more than Henry. There is no beginners group at the club but, because there are quite a lot of them, the boys are split into rough age groups. Ability is totally mixed and from the start, everyone joins in with everything, so on day one Henry was playing in a game. It was only then that I realised that he did not even know that football was a game

played in two teams and that it mattered which goal you headed for if you got the ball. Watching him, I felt very nervous that his ignorance and inexperience would show him up and anger his team mates. He really was in at the deep end.

Henry had a multiple learning task before him. On the social level he needed to learn how to behave as a member of the club as well as a member of a football team. Physically he needed to get started on the skills that would allow him to become a useful player and intellectually he had to get to know the game of football; what the rules were, and how they affected him and the other boys both as individuals and as team players.

Henry's situation was a real-life example of discovery learning; one that is emulated by the teaching strategy of supplying the problem and the answer, leaving the learner to work out for themselves the connection between the two. The football game was going on all around him; his task was to uncover the structure, rules and techniques that determined the form of play. Henry's basic strategy over the first few sessions was to observe as much as possible by following the ball around the pitch without actually making any effort to come in contact with it. He was up with the action, blending in, but not making any real contribution. He was however, watching and listening and, as it soon became clear, he was also learning.

In a belated effort to fill in some of the gaps in his knowledge, Henry's mother attempted after the end of the first session to explain to Henry how football was played in teams and what it meant to be a team member. 'I already know' he told her. There seemed to be two possibilities as to how he might have picked up this essential piece of knowledge so quickly. He may have worked it out from the talk and behaviour of others as the teams were selected, took up their positions and played their matches. Or, he may have picked up the idea of teams from some other unknown source, perhaps through a story or a TV programme or just from casual talk. If this was the case then that limited amount of casually acquired knowledge must have been rushed to the forefront of his mind in order to help him make sense of the new situation. In either case, Henry had never played a team sport before so his understanding of what a team is and how it behaves would have been very limited and would have needed some off the cuff, fast thinking to make sense of what was happening. Whether he used one of these sources of information or even both, Henry had done some major working out. Like anyone in a new situation he must have been right on the edge of mental alertness, making use of all the information available to him and possibly also filling in the gaps with some imaginative guesswork. It might be important to note that he did not ask any questions. This may have been partly a social strategy in not wanting to openly admit his ignorance. On the other hand it may be that his intellectual effort was not being spent on articulating his thoughts. Perhaps it was just too early for that and his thoughts had not gelled into a coherence that could very easily be put into words.

That guesswork, as well as making use of what he could observe, was part of his strategy to gain understanding was revealed in his attitude towards a second puzzling aspect of the game. Again, his mother observed what happened.

> Watching from the sidelines, I began to wonder what the rules were when the ball was accidentally kicked off the pitch. Sometimes it was kicked back on, sometimes it was thrown back on and I could not work out how they decided which method to employ and which player should do this. Henry was also clearly not sure. The first week whenever the ball left the pitch he ran after it. When I asked him, he said you could have it if you got there first. By the second week he had stopped running after it, and when I asked him about the rule again, he said he did not know.

It seems that Henry had constructed a hypothesis based on common sense, had then seen this contradicted, and had been forced to begin reconsidering what was going on.

> We had videos on football skills and a couple of library books and Henry could always have asked one of the coaches, even if he preferred not to display his lack of knowledge to the other players. However he chose to work things out for himself rather than use any of these resources. His strategy continued as before; watching the others, following the ball, involving himself with cautious commitment and, eventually the difference between corner kicks and throw ins became clear in his mind to the extent that he could explain it to me a few weeks later.

Once the children all began attending the Saturday Soccer School (his sisters followed Henry to the club a few weeks later) the amount of football being played in the garden also shot up. During those early weeks when they were still very new to the club it was these garden games which really revealed how much they had all learned. For a start the games became more sophisticated than before with a pitch and goals and teams. Play was interspersed with arguments about fouls and penalties and whether or not the ball had left the pitch. They were all very involved in these practice sessions; showing off their new skills and knowledge and pursuing the ball with relentless effort. Everything that they had learned, including the intellectual dimensions of the game, was being rigorously tested in this safe and familiar environment. The contrast between their cautious attitude at the soccer school and their authoritative invoking of the rules at home showed how different the same person's knowledge might appear to be in different situations. It was also an important part of hammering out between them any remaining misunderstandings about the rules.

Using these methods of observation, hypotheses building, testing and refining, and trying out what they felt they had learned on each other, all three children acquired, within about three or four weeks, a working knowledge of football rules without having received a single direct explanation. At the same time, they had transformed themselves socially into members of the club, picking up the behaviour and practices needed to blend in. The situation is the only specific element in this tale of learning; the learning skills themselves are highly transferable and general ones and display many of the 'thinking skills' that are so elusively chased through the school curriculum.

Fantasy play

Children play imaginary games involving fantasy from the earliest years. The following is the story of a game that three older children played and is included in order to illustrate some of the intellectual challenges and learning opportunities of play. It all began one afternoon when the children, aged six, eight and ten, made a pretend house out of cushions on the settee in the living room of their home. They had a few props, including a teddy bear dressed in a T-shirt and a denim hat and some cups and plates to make a kitchen. Out of the idea of the made up house grew a game which is retold here in the words of one of the children who played it. For ease of reading the original manuscript, which was part child written, part dictated to an adult, has been reproduced here with conventional spelling and punctuation.

Mountain Game

Long, long ago, once upon a time there was a little village and next to the village there was a mountain. Half way up the mountain there was a little wood hut and in the wood hut lived three children. Their names were Ip, Dip and Sky. The three children also lived with their mother who always wore long gloves with spindly fingers. She had a denim hat that she always pulled down over her eyes. Although the children had never seen their mother's face they knew she loved them dearly.

One day the children's mother said, "Children today you must go down the mountain to the village school."

"But Mambo," the children said, for that is what they called her, "What are we to do in the village school and how can we get down the mountain?"

"Ah that is easy, follow the sun and you shall get down the mountain! When you come to the school tell the teacher that you have come to learn to read and write," Mambo said, and with that she got them clover and fish for lunch and good luck!

So the children set off down the mountain to the school. When they got to the school Sky said to the teacher, "We're here to learn to," then Dip said "read and write" and Ip said "our mambo told us to".

The teacher laughed, "Your mother told you to did she?"

"Our mambo," said Ip.

She laughed again and said 'Call me Mrs Molder children and what are your names?'

"Ip, Dip and Sky," the children said together.

"They're unusual names. I've not seen you before. Do you live in the neighbouring village or the big town Kereth-Borne?" said Mrs Molder.

"We live on the mountain," said Sky.

"We followed the sun down to the village," said Dip.

"Then we asked someone where the school was," said Ip.

Again Mrs Molder laughed and said, "I had better ring the bell and call the other children in from the playground and you'd better come too!"

When the class had assembled in the classroom the teacher told them that some new children had come to the school and that their names were Ip, Dip and Sky. At lunch break while they were eating their clover and fish a girl came up.

"You're eating grass and raw fish," she said and then, "what shop does your father work in?"

"What's a father?" asked Ip.

"Good gracious me don't you know what a father is! A father!" she said and went off. Five minutes later she came back with a whole group of children. "They do not know what a father is," she said. One girl with plaits and glasses stepped forward.

"You're the new ones aren't you? Who claim you live on the mountain! Who lives in a mountain hut? I listened to that whole conversation you had with Mrs Molder, I did!" she said. Then another child spoke. This time a fat boy with orange hair.

"You're stupid," he said, "like Becky says, who lives on a mountain? Who? Who? Who?"

Then another girl broke in,

"You and your silly Membi! She'll be a bear in five minutes!"

"Her name is Mambo and so what if she was a bear. She would still love us and we do live on a mountain! We do, we do!" said Ip and burst into tears.

"Cry baby!" said the boy.

That night after school the children went up the mountain crying.

"They're mean," said Ip.

"And we do live on the mountain," said Dip.

"And Mambo won't turn into a bear!" said Sky.

When the children got home again they told their Mambo exactly what had happened.

"We cried all the way home," said Ip.

"We do love you Mambo," said Dip.

"At the bottom of it I suppose is that you do not know what a father is," said Mambo sighing.

That night when Mambo came to tuck them up she said,

"I have missed you a lot today children and now this. But I shall tell. A father is someone who goes with a mother. I'm your mother. The children in the village call their Mambos mother we call our fathers Barbo. Your Barbo went away one day and hasn't come back since."

"Why no-," Ip started but Mambo interrupted.

"Remember talk is dangerous! Now good night," with that she kissed all in turn and left the room.

"I didn't know we had a Barbo," said Ip.

"Neither did I," said Dip.

"Talk is dangerous," said Sky. So they all went to sleep.

The next day when they were climbing down the mountain Sky said "We're different to everyone else, aren't we?"

"I suppose so," said Dip.

"But doesn't everyone live in a wood cabin like us?" said Ip.

"I don't know," said Dip.

The children kept going to school every day for some time. Every day they realized that it was not the rest of the class that were different – it was them! On one occasion Becky's Mambo collected her from school without wearing a denim hat pulled down over her eyes. The children were shocked to see her face. They thought all Mambos wore denim hats pulled down over their eyes. Another time one of the children's friends from school invited them to a party Their house was completely different to the log cabin.

"It can't be right," said Dip that night, "they don't live like us."

The children's suspicions grew – why was their family so different to everyone else's?

One night when the children couldn't sleep they all decided that it would be worth a trip down to the cellar. It was very dark and the children thought about turning back but decided it would be best to stay. As they got further into the cellar Ip got more and more scared. Dip took him back whilst Sky searched on. A few hours later Sky came back with some clothes and a book. She opened the book and said,

"Look at this!'

Inside were some pictures of a bear and a man dressed in fine clothes.

"But who is it?' said Dip looking at a picture of the bear and the man getting married.

"You don't think do you?" said Sky

"No," said Dip, "No."

"But it is very odd – we even look different! I mean it could be possible!" said Sky.

"Don't be silly! Look Ip's already asleep. Let's see if we can too," Dip said pulling the covers over her.

"But don't let Mambo see the book and we mustn't let anyone see

Mambo's face. There's a reason why she wears that denim hat. Reasons," said Sky

"Yes," said Dip, "anyway night."

"Night," said Sky.

Nothing really changed at school for the next few weeks until Mrs Molder suddenly out of the blue said that they were going to learn to write. Ip, Dip and Sky loved writing. At night they would write notes to each other in bed. Until one night Ip said.

"This is too hard without Mrs Molder to help."

"I know," said Sky, "let's make our own alphabet."

"Yes," said Dip.

Sometimes Sky and Dip would stay up long after Ip had fallen asleep writing to each other. They would usually write about what they would do if their Mambo found the book. They always hid it under the bed covers but one day the children woke up late and had no time to make their beds. It was only when they got to school that they remembered the book. When they came back from school Mambo looked angry. At bed time she said to the children,

"You have been down to the cellar!"

"No we haven't Mambo," said Ip, who was too little to know not to tell lies.

"Then where did the book come from?" said Mambo, producing the book.

"We are very sorry Mambo," said Sky.

"We didn't mean to be naughty," said Dip.

"Soz," said Ip.

After Mambo had left the room, Sky said, "Never tell lies Ipomas."

"And we shouldn't ever wake up late," said Dip.

"Soz," said Ip again.

One day after school, whilst Mambo was in her room there was a knock on the door. Sky answered to see a man dressed in ragged clothes who said,

"I am a friend of your mother's, although you don't know me. Could you call her?"

"No," said Sky, "she does not want to be disturbed."

"Sorry," said the man and left. Unbeknown to the children, Mambo was looking from the window and saw the ragged man leaving. She said nothing to the children, but her heart leaped inside her.

A few days later, whilst they were at school waiting for lunch break to be over, Ip tripped and fell over whilst playing tig with his friend. Sky called Mrs Molder who said that Ip needed to go home and could the girls show her where they lived.

"No, no," said Dip, "we'll take him."

"Well," said Mrs Molder, "it would be better if I came too, but you can come with your brother if you like. Now then Sky can you show us the way to your house?"

"Up the mountain, towards the sun," said Sky reluctantly.

Mrs Molder had found Ip, Dip and Sky's family rather strange for a while now. She saw her opportunity now to call the school social worker and together they could investigate. Just after Mrs Molder and the social worker had emerged from the school door, they saw Sky disappearing up the mountain. But before Sky could reach the top she needed to stop and catch breath and before she could reach the hut Mrs Molder, the social worker, Ip and Dip were close behind her. Sky ran to the door of the log cabin and began to bang on it. Suddenly the door flew open and there stood Mambo. She expected the same visitor as a few days before, her head was bare and her face clear to see. Mambo was a bear. The social worker, breathless from the climb, looked up into the furry face. Before Ip, Dip or Sky could catch breath, Mambo shouted at them to follow her. Without hesitating the children leaped onto their mother's back and she set off sure footed and nimble as a wild animal leaving Mrs Molder and the social worker gazing after them with dumbfounded faces.

As they set off down the mountain, Ip shouted out,

"Hey! There's that man!" and sure enough the ragged man was running towards Mambo.

"It's your Barbo!" Mambo shouted with tears in her big brown bear eyes.

Finally the family was reunited forever. Later when they had found a place to sleep Mambo and Barbo explained to the children that many years ago, Barbo had been taken away because men and bears were not allowed to marry. Mambo had been forced to hide and give birth to her cubs in secret. Now at last they could be together again. (14)

The story of Mambo and her family, of their trials, their troubled past and the way in which they came to understand each other and their circumstances, emerged over the course of a few weeks. As the game moved along ideas were taken up, tried out, incorporated or abandoned. At one stage, for instance, an evil frog lived in the cellar and a mysterious net maker worked to make a net in which it could be caught, but as the play continued ideas were weeded out, some becoming minor subplots, some fading altogether as the overriding themes of the game emerged. Looking back over the game, the outstanding themes which had captured the children's imaginations were the meaning of being different, a mother who loved her children but lived with a dreadful burden, self-discovery and the uncovering of secrets at the heart of what they knew best. At the centre of the action lay the events that would first drive the children to uncover their true identity and then challenge them as to whether they would follow their old loyalties even in the face of the shocking knowledge they had so recently uncovered. Mountain Game had turned from some fairly idle fun into a piece of creative construction that evoked and explored some serious, even gripping, social and emotional questions. Its later state of permanence as a written story is an unusual one for a game. Writing the story down occurred either as the result of a suggestion or simply through a whim and allowed the game to grow yet further into a different kind of project. In its written form, Mountain Game has become something that can be speculated on and analysed although it has necessarily lost the flexibility of play. When the children began playing the game they had no conscious aim of creating a story; they were just playing a game from moment to moment, shuffling ideas about the family that lived in the settee house and what they might be doing that day. As the game deepened it began to take on its own life through its characters and through its plot. The children could no longer freely decide what would happen next, they had to begin considering what had happened previously, the emerging character traits of the family and how these would influence what happened next. Playing the game became a way of discovering the next stage of the story.

Mountain Game built on many levels and made many demands of those who took part in it. First of all there was the social collaboration necessary to playing together. The three of them had to work together, agree on characters, who would play who and how they would take it in turns to give voice to Mambo who was a dressed up teddy bear. They had to work out times in which they were all free and willing to play and they had to agree on the broad general direction of what would happen next and how they would conduct the play in practical terms. The course of the game needed to be discussed and consensus reached. Ideas were presented, mulled over, objections were raised or expansions made and finally the ideas were rejected or accepted, refined and put into practice. Sometimes they would backtrack over a piece that had been played but somehow did not satisfy by saying to each other 'pretend that bit didn't happen'.

Over and above this level of cooperation, the internal logic that would create a meaningful story, as opposed to merely a group of co-existing characters, had to be developed. As the game became more serious it needed to be talked over and decisions made. How would the children be feeling as they gradually gained the means to assess their own lives? How would Mambo be feeling as she saw her children gaining their independence? Had this been her intention all along? What happened as the situation gradually swung from one in which Mambo had protected her children to one in which the children needed to protect her? The answers to these questions lay to a large extent within the game itself, with understanding the characters and their motives so that they could react logically to their situation. For this the children needed to put themselves into the heads of the people they were playing. The more they could become these people the better the game would be in terms of both excitement and realism. As one of the children playing put it when discussing play in general,

It depends how much you believe in the character that you are playing with because you can say, I know we'll go and make so and so do this, it is more, what does so and so want to go and do now ... the thing is, to enjoy a game I think you have to have some kind of character that you can rely on.

Deciding what would happen next also drew on areas of understanding that lay outside the game. Issues rose up quite spontaneously through Mountain Game. These obviously included bullying, prejudice, the experience of being different, the limits of family loyalty, privacy, what it means to keep a secret and so on. The game in no way set out to explore these things but when they emerged as part of the story, experiences of, or ideas about these issues could be brought to bear on what might happen next. How far elements from their own lives or ideas from reading or from talking to other people might be incorporated in a game could be very flexible and depend on the degree of interest in the subject in question as well as on the game itself. Playing always allows for undesired elements to be pretended away or ignored, however it was clear that, at least in this case, working a path through some of the difficult ideas raised in Mountain Game was not an optional extra, it was integral to the game.

Mountain Game was clearly a fantasy and everyone involved knew that it was not an attempt to emulate real life yet it is shot through with real-life elements and ideas. Creating a fantasy imposes a discipline which is, in many ways, harder than simply following the dictates of real life. Fantasy has to have parameters or it would run the risk of sliding into chaos with no means of controlling the action. The basis of the story as it finally emerged is that of a talking bear who has had children with a human man and is now bringing up these unlikely cubs in a no-mans land between two societies. That part was pure fantasy but it did not confer licence on the rest of the story. The possibility that a fairy might come and wave a magic wand to take away their troubles or that the children could all turn into gnomes or wake up from a dream did not seem to exist. Instead a level at which the suspension of disbelief could come to rest had to be constructed within the fantasy setting. Parameters had to be negotiated which would contain the fantasy and allow it to co-exist with the rules that govern normal understanding. As one of the children themselves put it when discussing fantasy in general:

It's a fantasy with boundaries like we ... would just say that couldn't happen because although it's a fantasy it's a fantasy with limits.

Mountain Game was, on many levels, an exercise in creative thinking and development of narrative. It drew together diverse thinking skills such as exploring ideas, problem solving, thinking a situation through and putting yourself in the position of another person and seeking out their motives and needs. It was also just a game, one in a long string of games that these three played and enjoyed over the years. The appeal of play is built on both these levels; the challenge and the fun combined.

These two very different examples offer us a glimpse of some of the intellectual busyness that can accompanies children's play. In the first, it is intended and expected that the children will somehow 'pick up' what they need to know to play football simply by joining in. The adults running the club must have seen this kind of learning over and over again and found it to be effective for the club's needs. As well as being an example of children employing their own intellectual resources, this example also illustrates how simply being included in a group or community who behave in a particular way can induce learning. The second example of play is perhaps most enlightening for the way in which it reveals the self-imposed intellectual effort of 'just' playing. The children actually wanted to think about and become intellectually involved with the ideas they had raised for themselves. As one of the children put it 'play's fun because it is interesting'; in other words, the intellectual stimulation is integral to play's appeal.

Chapter 8

Reading

Learning to read is a critical step in the development of the primary aged child. Those who cannot master this skill with reasonable success by the age of about seven are left lagging behind in the educational system simply because subsequent progress across the curriculum depends on children's ability to read and write at an acceptable level. Failure to read often spells a downward spiral in which children may never recover the ground that widens out between them and their peers (Morag Stuart, cited in McMillan and Leslie, 1998). Even more critically perhaps, late reading is perceived as a sign of general lack of intellectual development. Alarm bells are sounded for those not reading by the standard age and special measures taken, followed by psychological assessment for those whose 'failure' persists. Not surprisingly therefore, overseeing the learning of reading has become an angst-ridden process for parents and teachers.

Reading not only lies at the heart of the primary curriculum but also constitutes the most intense area of educational research (Fischer, 2003). Despite this, no lasting consensus has been reached on the best way to go about teaching it. Preferred methods of teaching in school have come and gone and come again. According to Fischer 'the past two centuries have known hundreds of successful methods for teaching reading' (p. 324). Comparisons between methods have always been with large numbers in order to establish validity but the very desirable goal of dealing with individual variation, pinpointing which ones will work for whom has remained an elusive business. In the previous study of home-educating methods, even those parents who favoured a more structured approach, rarely stuck to one method (Thomas, 1998). Though most did not have any professional training in the teaching of reading they had the confidence to be quite pragmatic and flexible in their use of methods, based on an extensive knowledge of their children. This meant that parents often changed methods with the same child at different stages and sometimes used different methods with different children in the same family.)

In this chapter we explore how children learn to read when they are informally educated. The expectation that children should read by age seven is so strong that even some of the most 'informal' parents felt a need to teach the skill, especially if their children were approaching this age. However where children resisted, parents, in keeping with their child-led philosophy, reluctantly tended to back off so that many children learned to read 'late' by school norms. Resistance to being taught and late reading both featured in the earlier research (Thomas, 1998). We describe these aspects of informally learning to read before dealing with learning processes.

Resisting attempts to teach reading

There is considerable pressure on children and their families to get children reading as soon as possible. Children out of school may be largely unaware of this pressure but their parents are not. For home-educating parents, as for the parents of school-educated children, reading constitutes the major educational headache. It was the one area in which a number of parents felt the need to intervene and offer direct, purposeful instruction, particularly where children were not reading by the standard, school-dictated age of seven. However the outcome of parents' best efforts in this direction was rarely successful. Children frequently resisted any form of structured teaching and parents, despite their anxieties, usually ended up acknowledging their children's choice and giving up.

> He learned to read when he was eight. Everyone assured me that he would learn to read. I had a real problem with this. I love reading and we read to him all the time but he wasn't the slightest bit interested, so when he was six I had a go at teaching him and he was in tears in five minutes, we were both in tears. (9)

> He didn't read till quite late, probably around ten. At that stage I was quite worried about it and tried to teach him to read a lot but he just wasn't interested in it. (7)

> I actually started teaching [her] to read when she was six, using a reading scheme that a friend of ours had given us. They are actually really good stories. Some of the reading schemes I've seen are actually rubbish. It never went very well. She was always very resistant. She got more and more resistant. We kind of staggered on for a few months and then I called a halt. It wasn't going anywhere at all. So we just left it. (6)

> I tried to teach her phonics but she wasn't interested at all ... I tried and tried with three letter words just changing the vowels in the middle to

make different sounds, but she just didn't seem interested in the concept at all. (20)

The older boy, he was not reading when he was six and I was going, 'Oh my God!' because [his sister] was reading when she was four and I was thinking, 'I have a problem here' and I tried doing flash cards and after a few weeks he actually said to me, 'Do not waste your time. Leave me alone, I am not doing this thing.' So I stepped back for six months or so. (16)

We tried to teach her to read, not against her will, it wasn't like 'we've got to sit down and read now', it was when she wanted to and I would say, 'shall we read a book together? Do you want to read it?' But it didn't seem to work, well it worked a bit with her, she got to a certain level but I think what happened in retrospect was that we were pushing her beyond where she was naturally and it didn't help her to read in the long run, it didn't help at all. (21)

Clearly these periods of teaching must have added to children's overall literacy experiences but despite the fact that this teaching was on an individual basis and often using professional teaching material, most parents described their efforts at structured and sustained teaching as making no significant difference to their children's abilities. There were however, a couple of exceptions to this though, in both cases it was the children who requested assistance.

So about the age of six or seven [he] said he wanted to read and I asked him how he wanted to do it. I said I could easily do that with him and the best way was to get books that interested him and I showed him the different kinds of books and he chose them – a Ladybird scheme. We did that for ten minutes every night for about six months till he learnt to read. (1)

I made an attempt to teach her to read with learning books and we weren't getting anywhere so I dropped it and we had another couple of weak attempts at getting her to read every day and we weren't getting anywhere and then when she was ten she wasn't happy with her reading and she was reading very little and she wanted to do something about it. She wanted some help but she didn't want it from us, she was very clear on that. So we had a friend who had been a primary teacher who had retired early because of stress and she did weekly lessons with [her] for about nine months and she was the one who identified her as being dyslexic so we weren't surprised and she helped her a lot with her confidence. But she said [she] had to read for ten minutes every day with us at home so we did actually do ten minutes of reading together at home fairly reliably for that nine months and that got her to functional literacy. She is still a very slow reader but she functions as a reader and she does read for pleasure which is unusual for dyslexics because it is such a struggle. (26)

Only one parent described imposing a sustained and successful programme of deliberate teaching. This happened after previous attempts had ended in the same kind of failure as many of those quoted above, the difference may have been that on this final, successful push the child seems to have been reasonably self-motivated, at least up to a point.

[He] was a late reader and, having had two children who were early readers, [we] found late reading hard to accept and hard to understand. I've made some attempts to introduce some phonics on several occasions, made an effort to do five minutes of reading a day with him. Generally he's said he doesn't like it, resisted it, and I get the message and back off. At the start of this year I was doing a major panic thinking, 'He's nine and a half and the government is changing the laws on home education. If we are going to be inspected and so on, [he] had better be able to read.' So I started on a determined phonics programme of 30 minutes a day. I talked to him about 'cracking the code' and told him that if he learnt the code he would be able to read anything he liked. He was very keen to read and cooperated up to a point. We persisted with that for a couple of weeks and his reading vastly improved and then, recognizing that I had reached the unwanted teaching stage, I backed off again. (5)

So-called 'late' readers

Some children did learn to read early by school standards, but many were spread out in the seven to twelve age range and a few were even older than this. Parents were by no means immune to the educational and social pressures on children to begin reading as soon as possible and some were frustrated or puzzled that their children took an apparently long time to get interested in literacy.

At the time when the children were learning to read and write I can remember thinking, gosh our kids don't seem very interested in this at all. We read obviously a lot to them and they loved it but they didn't seem to want to do it themselves. (21)

I imagined her learning to read about six or seven really, I don't know why, and we did a lot of games and things but she wasn't really interested. She wanted to write, she'd get me to write books, stories but she'd get me to do the writing. (20)

> *Father*: One thing that is quite odd about literacy with them is that you know how they always say that one of the best ways of becoming literate early on or fairly early on ... is to have parents who read all the time, books about the house, reading stories to them and so forth, well all of that happened but they seemed to take a very long time to become interested in reading which I thought was quite odd.
> *Mother*: It was our expectation that they would be reading from the age of five because we both were. I struggled with that because I thought 'why aren't they? Why don't they want to?' (15)

Unlike in school however, 'late' reading did not appear to disadvantage these children in any way. They were all able to get on with other things that interested them by employing, as one father put it, 'the verbal, the visual and the hands on' as their learning methods. The explanations for reading at a later age are potentially many. One possibility is that children at home are simply not under pressure to start reading and have the freedom to wait until they are self-motivated to learn. This was the reason most frequently cited by parents, who often saw a specific motivating factor that galvanized their children into reading at a given point.

> Anyway, the catalyst in the end was Harry Potter No. 6. I was reading to her and she got fed up waiting for me to get around to it. She just picked it up herself and started reading it. That was the catalyst. That was the change then and she's now reading *Lord of the Rings* and *Oliver Twist*. She reads about five or six books at once. She dips into them and they can be factual books as well as fiction books. I have no worry at all with her reading now. (6)

> Nothing really seemed to stick until he wanted to do it and that was the Sonic comics and that was also about the time that we got the first computer and it was to do computer games really, he wanted to know all about computer games and that's when he started reading. (20)

> When he started to play the Rhunescape, that was when he started to learn to read and write. He was about seven or eight. And it happened almost overnight, it was really quick. (21)

Children may not perceive a need to read if they are busy with other things and have adults or older children around who are willing to fulfil their literacy needs.

> She's concentrated on doing her own thing for ten years really and now she's reading or beginning to read, she doesn't read quite fluently yet. (20)

[She] isn't phased out by the fact that she can't read. She goes to Woodcraft Folk and other things where reading could be involved and she doesn't have a problem with saying to one of the other children, 'what does it say?' (24)

We always read books to them, up until they got too old for it, every day we'd read to them. We got through masses and masses. (21)

As we have said, most parents worried if their children were not reading by the age of seven. However, having the experience of one child reading 'late' meant that they could be much more relaxed about a younger sibling's progress.

He was 10¼ when he started reading. The first book he read was *Swallows and Amazons* by Arthur Ransome. That's a pretty solid book. It's 300 pages and it's a novel. It's got big words in it. He had never read a book before, even the children's books, *Dr Seuss*, phonics, starters, all of which we had lying around which I presented to him on odd occasions. He loved being read to but he didn't really enjoy even hearing those children's books. I tried not to let it concern me. I'd been doing support work within the home-schooling communities for about ten years since [he] was five. We'd do workshops with parents on trusting your children – they are going to learn to read – it's OK. Let them take their time. Until he was actually reading I did feel somewhat of a fraud but I had read of very many cases where that had happened especially with boys and especially with boys who spoke late. He was never very verbal, verbally fluent. I knew all of this in my head and the panic attacks you experience as a parent I tried to dismiss. [His younger brother] learned to read … in the same fashion. You think there is something about the brain development in those kids that made them ready to learn to read. Because [his older brother] progressed like that I never had the slightest qualm about him and he just learned. (3)

Not only does late reading at home appear to hold no knock on educational disadvantage but it also seems to have no long-term consequences for reading ability. Many children, who learned late, made up the ground in a remarkably speedy fashion once they did begin to read. In order to give a sense of individual variation and the varied paths to reading here are just a few examples of learning to read at a later age that we encountered.

At nine and a half he really enjoyed street signs. In six months he was reading signs on cornflakes and packaging. He wanted to know what they said. He also got interested in advertisements. When he was nine and a half he was writing [MOT] instead of [TOM] so we called him [MOT].

You're faced with a problem and you've got to get over it. There was a little bit [of worry] in the background. Outside people asked why he couldn't write. They said you've got to get the problems seen to early on. Then, at ten he was reading from the newspaper. Two months later he started to learn Spanish. It really puzzled me. He was reading an adult textbook. We chewed on this for a while. I was mystified. At school he'd have been told how far behind he was. (11)

He was so anti anything which looked academic and clearly found it difficult that it was more important to have him being a happy child who was loving life than it was to be upset because we were trying to do the stuff that was difficult. And I guess by the time he was 11 and then began to read and I went Oh! Oops! So he didn't do it at seven or eight. He did it at 11... He was the child we'd give a book to for his birthday; he'd go 'Yuk! Not a book!' I gave up giving books for gifts ... I guess I was then in that process of just letting them learn and encouraging them and supporting them. [The next one] didn't read until he was 12 and [the youngest, now aged 11] is a non reader. (2)

He taught himself to read with Sonic comics I think when he was about nine or ten. (20)

And in fact they didn't start reading until well after the normal school time, about eight or nine before they were fluent readers and after the initial worries, we didn't worry any more and in fact it is only my daughter who is now 15, 15 a few weeks ago, it is only now that she is really reading a lot for pleasure. Before she would read but you wouldn't find them buried in a book. (21)

I think it was probably seven, he wanted to get 'Sonic the Comic', he wanted this weekly comic and he had that and he leaped from there, I'm not quite sure what the time scale was, maybe six months later, he wanted the little chapter books that they produced. So from the comic, I don't know what reading age it would count as, to something that was maybe a quarter of an inch thick and a series of ten of them and he went from those to reading the Red Wall books with nothing in between. (16)

He was always a dreamer. He never wanted to learn to read. Probably didn't even know when his birthday was. Till he was about 12 he always wanted to watch *Star Wars* and stuff, wrapped up in it totally. He loved Lego, loved playing on the trampoline. He was more of a boy boy; nothing to do with academics at all. He never wanted to write. He didn't read till quite late, probably around ten. (7)

Informal processes in learning to read

None of the above actually explains how these children learned to read though teaching, at least of the formal kind, seems to play, at the most, a very minor role. So what in fact is going on?

Fischer (2003) lists a number of understandings that children need before they begin to read including recognizing and being able to name letters, being able to distinguish different sounds in speech, the ability to isolate words within speech and then added to this a bunch of psychological factors including memory, general language ability and intellectual development, attention, and left–right orientation. To these Weinberger (1996) adds a social and cultural dimension. Literacy appears in real life in a variety of contexts and settings; prior knowledge about these situations is not only an aid to decoding print but gives the written word meaning once it is decoded. In order to actively derive meaning from print the reader needs to be able to relate what is read to other experiences and knowledge. In other words reading does not exist as a skill in isolation though this is how it is often treated in school; it is connected to language, to life, to culture and experience.

During the 1960s and 70s the belief that children, given the right sort of environment, would pick up reading for themselves and would start reading when they were 'ready' became a fashionable idea. It has since been largely dismissed as a teaching method and as a philosophy. David Bell, chief inspector of schools in England, for instance argued that such methods, based on the 'totally soft centred belief that children would learn if you left them to it [are] plain crackers' (Smithers, 2004). We take the opposite view. Modern life takes place within a vast sea of written material that surrounds us, is pertinent to virtually every situation and which plays a part in so many activities. To us, it seems impossible to overemphasize the influence this has over how and why children learn to read. Long before children begin to read for themselves the experience of living in a literate culture and being surrounded by people for whom reading is not just a meaningful, but a vital, skill endows children with an implicit understanding of what literacy is and how it is used. Research into the lives of pre-school children such as that of Stainthorp and Hughes (1999) or Weinberger (1996) describes how rich this stream of experience can be. Words are literally everywhere; children are surrounded by advertisements, street signs, junk mail, catalogues, books, television titles, cards, T-shirts with slogans on them, shopping lists, instructions, magazines, bus destinations – the list goes on and on. Reading is relevant to virtually every single experience from walking down the street, to playing a board game, visiting the doctor, going swimming, using the computer, etc. etc. Home-educating parents attested to this constant literacy input.

I think the fact that we do read, as in the society that we are in at the moment does read, so there is an understanding of the fact that these symbols or whatever, these squiggles are words and that they are in our everyday life, like the door over there says 'Main Hall' and you can work out, because it is a label for something and that you know that there is a word for something which would obviously have a meaning. And I think that there is an input without realizing that there is an input. (24)

Weinberger uses the term 'emergent literacy' to describe the growing understanding of literacy as children experience it from babyhood onwards. The way that children encounter literacy on a day-to-day basis is highly contextualized and that context helps children understand what they are seeing, whether it is the name of the cereal on the packet, a familiar favourite story, prompts on the computer, the title of a TV programme, seeing the same letters in different words, recognizing your own name or that of a shop, pretend reading, making a birthday card. The list can go on and on and every one of these experiences adds incrementally to literacy awareness and understanding. This context is not a separate 'background' to literacy contained in graded reading material, rather it is an essential element of what literacy is and how we use it. For some of the parents with younger children such encounters were part of the here and now.

He has started to get interested [in reading]. He loves books, all three of them do. B will sit and look through books. He recognizes his name and if it is written he knows what it says, he'll say it's T for [his name]. When I was writing a card from B, he knew and said it's B for [his sister's name] and that was the first time that he had said that as well. He's just beginning to pick it up. (17)

He's actually starting to read and he can spell his own name. He can write his own name. He can do yes, no, and on, off and he knows a lot of his letters because we sit at the keyboard sometimes and he wants to look up things on the search engine and I say he can type them in. I say what line it's on and he usually gets it. (6)

We noticed a big improvement, by the time the end of the day came along on her birthday, she was opening the cards and saying, 'this says "happy birthday"' and recognizing what people had written. (17)

It seems that the beginnings of literacy within a literate society consist only of very small incremental steps. The most important of these is the child's initial recognition that letters are different to other symbols and patterns that they see around them, that they re-occur in different variations and above all that they are meaningful to other people. The first time that a child points to some print and asks 'what does this say?' an important breakthrough in becoming literate has taken place. It is however, something that happens so early and so easily that most parents fail to notice it. Certainly, it is accepted that children beginning school will already know that letters are an abstract means of representing other things. If they did not come to this recognition for themselves it would be far too complicated to explain. The home-educated children were not exceptional in their early learning about literacy through day-to-day life but were able to continue building on this after their school peers were moved on to more deliberate reading schemes, books and targets.

Stainthorp and Hughes (1999) in a study of children who learn to read before starting school regarded them as being very exceptional. They conclude, like David Bell (cited in Smithers, 2004) that 'people do not achieve literacy simply by being in a literate environment. The majority of people need to be specifically taught, over a number of years, how to read and how to spell' (p. 9). However, the experience of many home-educating families contradict this conclusion. As we have seen above, children often rejected being taught but then learned, under their own steam or by asking for assistance when they needed it, at a time that suited them. The difference between these children and those studied by Stainthorp and Hughes is that their pre-school children had only a very short time in which to accomplish independent reading. Once they started school, the teaching of reading would become a matter of course and what they had already achieved alone and might have continued to achieve given the opportunity, could not be known. The home-educated children on the other hand continued as they had begun, in absorbing the meaning and practice of reading from life around them.

Building up and taking off

Some parents were able to continue tracing their child's route into literacy.

> It is coming naturally and she is taking more in, I've watched her walking from somewhere to somewhere and she is looking at the words on things, doors, windows whatever, whereas she wasn't before. And she says things, I hear her talking under her breath and reading things, although she won't admit to it and I think that she is finding it easier. (24)

> And when she was writing 'happy' and I was spelling it out for her she said, 'I know there's double p in happy' so she knows some things although we haven't made a point of it. She knows by seeing us doing it and birthdays and Christmas. (17)

She likes picture books and she'll make up her own stories. Sometimes she'll read labels or signs. On the way here today she worked out how you spell Tom and she'd never seen Tom written before but she worked it out for herself … she does just build up gradually. Six months ago she had no concept of letter sounds but now she can work out how to put words together that she has never seen before. (17)

Both have gone through patches where they read all the road signs when you are going somewhere. [One of them] in particular will pick up any package offer off the table, spell it out and read it and say why does that say whatever. What does that say? (2)

There were a lot of skills being absorbed towards reading and sometimes you are not even aware of what they are. There is the very simple one of driving in the car and I can remember [her] picking out a word like Statoil and wanting to know what it was and every time we passed something she was probably doing the recognition thing. (4)

Word recognition, things in shops and all of that and that was all happening … I think she could read Shell and Esso. (6)

For some reason, all of a sudden, he liked the word 'extra'. I remember as a little boy, the word extra thrilled him to bits and he'd spend hours going through the newspaper and he had an 'extra' collection. It was extraordinary. He loved the word. (7)

At this stage there seems to be a grey area as children move towards full literacy. A reading scheme would, at least on its own terms, be able to pinpoint a child's level of literacy but without this convenience the question of when a non-reader becomes a reader is much harder to answer. Many parents recognized that non-reading children knew a lot about reading and were in fact able to read in particular contexts. The speed with which many children moved from being apparently non-readers to reading anything that they chose, suggests that they already knew a large amount and that the final stage was simply a pulling together and refining of the knowledge and skills they already held.

I think she realized that she had picked up a lot of words from the computer, that she could already read; she said that she couldn't read but actually she was reading a lot, you know the words that are always on the computer, 'yes', 'no', 'exit' all these small words she could recognize immediately. (20)

She sometimes says, 'Let me have a look', or she'll say something, she'll read things and then say, 'does it say that?' and I'll say, 'Course it does, you just read it.' 'Oh I don't really ...' (24)

The comment from one child looking back on her experiences of learning to read also bore out this idea. It seemed that she was actually reading quite a bit before becoming a 'reader' in the full sense of reading books or other conventional reading matter.

[*Daughter* (aged 13)] I don't remember reading much until maybe about nine or ten. I started trying to read things a little bit and in between that time – Dad was right – I read a lot of things, I read street signs or I read shops in passing or if I was in a shop I would read ingredients on the back of a packet. Or things that I actually saw in front of me and read. At home I really didn't really need to read and I didn't see the point in it particularly at that point which is why I probably didn't read so much. (6)

For other children though even these kinds of clues seemed to be missing. Literacy just seemed to arise complete and whole; leaving even those closest confounded as to how it had all happened.

... one day when he was barely four ... up to now there'd been no indication that he even knew his letters. He said I'm going to read you a book. It was a little board book about Thomas the Tank Engine which we knew he loved. He read it to us. We thought that's an accident. He's memorized it. Then very quickly he progressed from there to chapter books. So we knew it wasn't an accident. So just because he'd been read to, I think, and seen us read and watched us work with [his sister] with her reading. From the outside it looked like he was a spontaneous reader. (8)

I honestly don't know to this day how he learned to read. Sometimes he used to sit in bed with us when [his brother] was reading and it was bed time when we read. One day when he was eight, he was reading a Tintin book and I thought he was looking at the pictures and he was laughing. What's so funny? Is the picture funny? 'No, the joke is ...' and he read the joke and I said: 'Well how do you know that?' And he read it and he started reading the book out loud to me and I thought Wow! How on earth has he done it? Where he got it I don't entirely know. (1)

I knew that he knew a few words but I wasn't really aware that he could read. We got a book out of the library one day and I read it to him and he asked for it again so I read it to him again and then he took it off me and he read it himself. It had 70 pages. He could just read it. I was just astounded. I had no idea he could do that. (5)

I think [she] mostly learnt to read by herself actually. (6)

She found some more interesting books when she had been about a year out of school and then reading seemed to come within a few months. She reads a lot of fantasy novels, adult stuff. (20)

Some parents rationalized this apparently baffling process, feeling that their children had been implicitly absorbing the meanings and conventions of literacy, often in ways and situations which did not involve their parents, certainly not directly.

The contribution of children's particular interests or hobbies

A lot of the time it seemed that children were implicitly absorbing from the environment around them. Neither they nor their parents were aware of an effortful or deliberately directed learning process though opportunities for extending literacy abounded. As has been already mentioned, for many children literacy was also facilitated by children's specific interests, leading to a desire to get reading for a particular purpose. This is intrinsic motivation of course as opposed to school where learning to read is an external requirement regardless of children's interests.

> … learning to read was an extension of singing. He was a very keen singer. In fact there's a children's singing group called The Wiggles. As a toddler, [he] was the biggest Wiggles fan in the world. He knew all the words to their songs. The boys spent hours watching the Wiggles videos, listening to the Wiggles tapes and CDs. The CDs had the words printed on the slicks and he wanted me to type out the words in big print for him. He made up a binder full of Wiggles songs and he taught himself to read from those. He knew what the words were. All he had to do was to figure out the one-to-one relationship. And all of a sudden he could read. (5)

> My son's current obsession is Yu-Gi-Oh cards which is just cards like Pokemon but more advanced and in actual fact what Yu-Gi-Oh has actually done for him is that it has improved his English reading, because there is tons to read and really complicated words. (23)

Although they don't have friends around physically as much as they would like, they are always in contact with them either on the internet, not so much on the phone, but usually instant messaging, chat rooms, I know school kids do this a lot as well and they have their home ed friends there and probably a few others and they spend a lot of time doing that and that's where they have learned their fluency in writing and reading. (21)

The Dungeons and Dragons, to really get into it, you need to read reference books. There are many reference books and they are like A4, half an inch thick, one on how monsters work, one on how something else works, one on how to be the person who runs the game for other people, there's volumes of this stuff and the more you know the more you have in your head about all the different rules and how they interrelate the more fun you can have. So when he realized that he needed to read these books to really get into this game, I think that was the motivation that really made him do it ... he started with those. There was a need and he found a route. (16)

When [he] was very small he was interested in numbers. He had a numbers book which he read and read and read. He knew all the numbers but at some stage he learnt the words that went with it. First of all he knew the numerals and then he knew the word that matched the numeral and then he picked up the other words on the page. He loved that book. (5)

His reading age is ahead of his chronological age, and he's done that all himself; he's not had any teaching. Hardly any help at all, occasionally he'll ask what a word is. He's self taught as far as reading goes. And, largely it has to be said, from computer games and manuals and things that he was really interested in reading for himself. (15)

He taught himself to read with Sonic comics I think when he was about nine or ten ... nothing really seemed to stick until he wanted to do it and that was the Sonic comics and that was also about the time that we got the first computer and it was to do computer games really, he wanted to know all about computer games and that's when he started reading. (20)

There is this wonderful thing in home education ... called Magic the Gathering ... a card game and they have to buy the cards. There is a certain element that if you have more money you can buy better cards but it's a strategy game, it's about understanding the possibilities of what you have in your hand but they've all got instructions and information on, and the motivation of playing with your friends that thing, you have got to be able to read those cards and that's what made him read. (16)

She's playing different computer games which she had previously avoided because there was too much reading involved. So perhaps because she wanted to play these games and [her sister] is not always around to help her or somebody else is not always around to help her she taught herself to read. (20)

What part do parents play?

We have already seen that very few of the parents attributed their child's reading success to being taught in the usual sense and yet, of course parents were not apart from what was going on. Again, in common with almost all parents, they provided specific resources that might encourage children to play with and become familiar with letters, words and sentences. This might be pens and pencils, paper, magnetic letters, board games, puzzles, letter racks, home-made materials. They also provided books, magazines and comics. They read aloud to their children as a matter of course, from babyhood until, and often beyond, the point when children became independent readers themselves.

They were raised on stories. L in particular had story after story. (15)

I read books to her all the time. (24)

I read out loud quite a lot, most of it fiction. (26)

We always read books to them, up until they got too old for it, every day we'd read to them. We got through masses and masses. (21)

She's always loved being read to, so I read lots of stories and she's surrounded by books. (17)

Reading aloud demonstrates a number of reading skills to children: how to handle books, where to start and where to finish reading, turning pages, finding page numbers, front to back and right to left orientation. It also introduces the idea of stories, what they are and how they relate to real life in different ways. Listening to stories helps children map their own experiences onto the written word so that what they are hearing makes sense to and holds meaning for them. It also introduces a feel for the flow of words, helping children to anticipate what may be coming next.

I think that if you've already heard a lot of literature then you are expecting the words, the flow of words. I would say that that is the most important thing: being read to and listening to tapes, watching television programmes and being totally absorbed in the words and the flow of the words. You're expecting certain words because you've heard them in context so many times. (20)

Reading was always an interest for them and they loved it and I think they just picked it up. And I think they probably, I don't know if S did or not, but sitting right next to me they probably followed the lines while I was reading. (21)

Although parents didn't teach in the conventional sense they provided innumerable casual opportunities to extend literacy during social conversation, playing word games and so on.

We used to walk along the street and try and pronounce number plates, that kind of thing. (26)

No way, shape or form would he sit still with a book. But we took trips into town and played games with road signs. (11)

Parents also provided assistance on an ad hoc basis. They helped with reading as requested, following the child's cue as to when and what they needed to know.

It's from everyday situations isn't it? We're not teaching her at the moment but there have been times when she has sort of shown more interest and wanted to and we've sat down with her and sounded words out with her but then she lost interest so we just left it. We very much do it based on her own interests, on a needs-to-know basis, she'll say what does this say and we'll just tell her rather than get her to sound it out. She just seems to be picking up more and more stuff like that. (17)

We have already noted how literacy is a facet of very many interests that might come a child's way. In supporting and encouraging these individual interests parents were also obliquely supporting the literacy aspects that would, somewhere, be part of them. Sometimes this might involve an act of faith on the parent's part, allowing their child to follow an interest, perhaps very intensively, even though its 'educational' worth might appear extremely small.

I had this woman from an LEA saying, 'Well I don't know how it works for you, but I would consider myself to be totally irresponsible if I just allowed my son to play with Yu-Gi-Oh cards all day. He'd have to do something constructive in the day.' ... It was only yesterday that I realized all the stuff that he'd got out of having these Yu-Gi-Oh cards and that my nervousness over the last two months where he's been obsessed with them is totally out of place because I should just have confidence that he knows what he is doing and he is moving forward in the way that is most appropriate for him. (23)

Finally, parents modelled manifold uses of literacy: writing shopping lists, doing crosswords, reading packages, following instructions, the many day-to-day tasks that involve reading but which do not spring to mind precisely because they are so commonplace. Being able to observe or to become in some minor way involved in their parent's literacy provides children with apprenticeship-style opportunities for furthering their own understanding. As one parent put it …

She watches other people, sees what they get out of being able to read. (24)

What part does reading play in the lives of home-educated children?

In school, as we have already noted, there is a lot of pressure on children to become fluent readers in the early years of their primary education. Based on what we have found this might be too early for some children who, having to struggle to learn to read, will be less likely to find it a pleasurable activity in its own right. Heavy emphasis on the formal acquisition of basic literacy at an early age may improve scores on school reading tests but also has the potential to turn children off reading for pleasure (Egan, 2005: xv). As Thomas (1998) found previously and this research confirms, home-educated children seemed to thoroughly enjoy reading and read for relaxation, for pleasure, for the excitement of it or even as an obsession:

> *Father*: When the Harry Potter books came out we read them to the children and then L in particular, she read them for herself, maybe a couple of years ago and now she has just re-read them all, very fast. That's exactly what has happened and she must have enjoyed them because she went straight from the end of one to the beginning of the next, including the great big fat ones. (21)

> *Mother*: But she got into books when she was nine and when she gets into a book she's really into it and can't put it down, she'll read it in a day or two. And then we'll all tend to read it, if it's really good. She'll say, 'you must read it as well' and we'll all read it. (21)

> My children have always read, will always be found with a book, they never leave the house without a book … We've actually had to ban books

from the car at the moment because we want the children to be in the car, looking out of the windows because we can say, 'where are we now?' and they won't know. ... I do think that at nearly 13, should know what's at the end of the road. (18)

Chapter 9

Writing

Like reading, writing encompasses a group of skills which need to be brought together. First, there are those of a technical nature which apply to handwriting and/or keyboard skills: spelling, grammar and punctuation. Second, there is the need to learn the conventions that govern the different formats such as letter writing, recipes, text messages and the different styles such as are associated with poetry, reports, prose and so on. Finally there is the sphere of individual expression; the creative side of writing in which, within the framework of the rules, the writer finds their own voice and is able to develop their own personal style. The journey from infant scribbles to competency along these three dimensions constitutes an intellectual challenge for both individuals and schools. Beard (2000) summarizes the task as follows:

> During the years between 3 and 13, writing skill can be transformed from the early scribbles of the pre-school child to the weekly production of dozens of pages of notes, essays, poetry and prose. This achievement by so many young people is easy to under-estimate. It represents growth along several linguistic dimensions: of broadly understanding the relationship between language and literacy, and of specifically fusing together spelling, vocabulary and grammar into a range of texts. Each type of text will have its socially valued features and traditions. (p. 1)

There is a strong expectation that children in school should start writing as soon as possible in parallel with learning to read. As with reading this is pretty much a necessity because the curriculum relies heavily on writing ability and written material is used as the major evidence that learning has taken place. From the age of six or seven onwards writing rapidly grows in importance across the curriculum with emphasis not just on content but also on the 'correct' handwriting style, spelling, punctuation and layout. Improvement is encouraged through spelling lists and practice in handwriting and punctuation exercises.

Ironically, little if any time is given to word processing or text messaging though as adults these will far outweigh handwriting in importance.

By contrast, it is hard to judge how much informally-educated children at home actually write. Our hunch is that most probably write far less than their schooled peers but there are some children who become hooked and turn into prolific writers. The amount of writing which takes place therefore probably varies considerably between individual children. This leads to the major difference between school and home; at home children only write when they need to or when they want to, rarely as an activity the sole purpose of which is to improve writing. So their writing is not contained neatly in a set of exercise books but scattered through their lives in the form of notes, lists, reminders, letters, emails, stories, captions, instructions and so on.

Despite its clear educational importance, most of the home-educating parents were far less concerned about learning to write than they were about learning to read. Perhaps, as these parents explained, they felt that after reading had been accomplished, writing would follow quite naturally.

> I always felt, once they'd learned to read, my feeling is you can do anything if you can read because reading is going to lead to writing at some point. If you can read fluently you are going to be able to separate out the letters and after a while he began to want to write. He didn't ask us really how to do that. (1)

> I don't remember teaching them how to write, I don't think [my partner] did. They just did it. There was no effort at all involved from our point of view. (21)

Fewer parents seemed to feel the need to intervene with writing than they did with reading, yet where this did happen the pattern of resistance followed very much the same path as for reading or other attempts at direct teaching.

> *Mother*: I want the girls to stay in control of their own destiny if you like. Where I question it is when perhaps they aren't meeting the targets that are there in the school world and the most visible one for me would perhaps be writing ... It is a worry that we have that there isn't enough maths going on, or enough writing. Yes, writing is another point. Both of them read and neither of them can write. They will write for their own purposes but I fear that the degree to which they will write is limited by their lack of facility, lack of practice.
> *Father*: So come January after one Christmas I said, 'We are going to keep a diary and you have to write each day the number of words which is your age'. They were seven and nine. That's not too much ... It lasted till about three quarters of the way through February and it was like pulling teeth. Finally, [one of them] threw down her pen and said: 'Never again'!

The worst part about it was it drove them to rebellion. It was a very bad experience ... (4)

Nevertheless, these children's writing did seem to develop. This is what their mother added to the transcript of the interview when it was sent to her for approval and amendment.

Ten days after the interview, [now aged 9 and 12] they put together almost entirely by themselves, a four page pull-out section for the [Home Education] Newsletter. Several hundred words of copy typed in and marked up. (4)

Once again we are faced with the question, if children are not being taught writing, how are they learning it?

Finding a different route to writing competence

As with reading, children at home have the opportunity to become aware of the uses of writing through the actions of the adults around them. Family life at home offers an abundance of situations in which writing is relevant: marking an important day on the calendar, having a go at the crossword, writing a birthday card as well as more formal types of writing such as letters and filling out forms. Children see adults writing shopping lists, notes to each other, jotting down reminders, using the computer. Here writing is found, not as a decontextualized skill to be practised for its own sake but as a cultural tool used for both pleasure and for getting important things done. Modelling of genuine reasons for writing surround children and provide the first materials from which an understanding of composition can begin to be built.

Children seeing adults writing may emulate their actions long before they understand either the purpose or the technicalities of what is going on. As a child, Alan Thomas recalls wanting to write a letter after watching his father doing so. He then filled a whole page with a continuous up and down stroke that resembled a series of the letter w. Being in a position to see how adults use, as well as perform writing, children begin to understand its purposes as well. Hall (1994) describes how pre-school children seize on paper, pens and pencils to make labels, signs, timetables and other props for their games. Already these children have grasped what writing is; they understand that it is used to communicate and are aware of some of the specific circumstances and ways in which this takes place. It is a small step for children to begin to incorporate into these purposeful scribbles the shapes of actual letters which they may have seen around them. Glenda Bissex (1980) who made a detailed analysis of how her son Paul learned to read and write, gives an example of a 'Welcome Home' banner made in her honour and consisting of partly invented and partly real letters.

Once even a modicum of competence has been attained, children write and use their writing for the same kind of purposes as do adults.

> She's forever writing things up – it might be scribble or it could be real words, depends. (24)

> He's not got to the stage yet where he wants to write much. He does write, he writes me notes and things like that and he writes down passwords for cheats on computer games. (23)

> I've noticed he's putting more and more labels on things. He spends a lot of time drawing. He puts labels and speech bubbles on his drawings. And he calls out: How do you spell Civil War? Then on the computer he's calling out: How do you spell General Custer? He also learns a lot by copying his brothers. He asks them for help and he copies what they do. (5)

> And he [the LEA inspector] said, 'Well when your children do writing would they be doing it in exercise books or on loose paper?' and I said, 'They only do purposeful writing; they write letters and lists and stuff that they want to write.' (26)

In this way, the different uses to which writing can be put are embedded in these children's writing practice from the very start. Children understand the purpose of what they are writing as they are doing it. As well as the more obvious notes, shopping lists, reminders and greetings cards we have come across menus for meals they are preparing, advertisements, 'for sale' leaflets, programmes for plays which they are putting on, comic strips, newspaper reports, games, instructions, songs and poems, readers for younger children, puzzles, stories as gifts which feature the recipient as a hero, codes, invented scripts and so on. The sheer variety of examples shows how children have picked up the diverse purposes to which writing can be put. It is also a chance to get to grips with writing conventions; a list is different in composition and layout to a greetings card or a story. Writing has different target audiences – whether it is solely for the writer's own use or intended to interest, entice or baffle another reader is a consideration which plays an important part in composition. Children are able to cultivate the ability to stand outside their own writing and see it from someone else's point of view – a very important aspect of composition that can make or break the significance of the written word.

Whilst some children took to writing others did not. Writing requires considerable effort and most adults do not write unless there is a need to. It is no surprise that some children might not want to write, or at least might not find all aspects of writing inspiring or attractive. The following shows how one child developed the creative aspects of writing well before she wanted to pursue the exacting technical side.

> She wanted to write, she'd get me to write books, stories, but she'd get me to do the writing ... sometimes months would go between one chapter and another and she'd see how her writing had changed, new ideas, new styles and things like that and poetry too, she'd [compose] poems and get me to write them down. I always tried to encourage her to write herself and then spell things, but I think she'd get impatient with it, it'd stop her flow of ideas, she didn't feel like combining the two. She found it just got in the way ... she makes up a lot of stories that she does not want to write down. She talks to herself a lot, in her own world, her own inventions and that can be for hours at a time. ... From the understanding point of view, she's very good, people remark on her vocabulary and some children say, 'Why do you use such long words?' and that's from listening to a lot of adult literature I think ... I think that a lot of learning is listening, which children in school perhaps don't have the time to do, they don't have the time to listen to stories for hours and hours ... (20)

Learning to write informally allows for this lopsided development to occur. Children in a literary environment do not have to write themselves in order to understand why other people write. Furthermore certain aspects of writing can be practised without taking on the full task from the very start. Examples like the one given above prompt the question of how far the actual practice of writing is essential in the early stages. Reading, listening to stories, overhearing and taking part in conversations all contribute to the development of narrative and description and enhance vocabulary and expression. Play provides the opportunity to create situations and characters and to pursue storylines, again without any actual writing taking place. Mercer (1995) recounts an instance in which he overhears his daughter (aged nearly 3) turning their conversation into a story by adding the words 'she said to her Daddy' (p. 6), after she had spoken to him. In his analysis of this incident he sees his daughter recasting her current situation into a narrative by using her experience of another type of language event (listening to a story). Such creative use of both language and experience is part of the process of self-expression and one of the skills of composition in writing. Yet it does not actually involve lifting a pen. The opportunity to talk, listen, play and use language in a variety of ways and in different situations may provide a stronger basis for writing competence than the production of large amounts of writing.

Technical aspects of writing

Whilst composition and understanding the conventions of composition are very important aspects of writing they need to be supported by technical skills if writing is to fulfil its communicative purpose. In school the emphasis on achieving this is through instruction, correction and practice; at home much less, if any of this goes on. External technical correction is often only provided at the child's own request when they have decided that there is a genuine need for accuracy for the sake of the recipient. This might be when writing an official letter or an important story. How correct children wanted their writing to be for its own sake varied quite a lot.

The result seems to be that standards of spelling, handwriting and general presentation, at least during the early years of writing can lag behind those expected of children in school. Professionals can be quite shocked at this lower technical standard if they come across it, as Alan Thomas found when, with a colleague, he was visiting a Local Authority official to request permission to interview home educators. During the course of the visit the advisor mentioned a recent inspection of a family and produced a piece of creative writing by an eight-year-old child which her mother had proudly produced for the occasion. The advisor was scathing. Obviously from a teacher's point of view it was unacceptable, written on a scrappy piece of paper, misspelt, poor handwriting, going in all directions, difficult to decipher. For those more familiar with the offerings of informal learning however, the writing appeared in a much more positive light. Alan and his colleague knew that this child would, in all probability, turn out to be a fully competent writer. Incidentally, there was no mention of the content of what the child had written. So how is competency in the technical side of writing achieved?

Spelling

In school, spelling is taught; at home it is learnt by a variety of means. An obvious and most efficient one is for children to ask parents to spell for them the words that they need as they need them.

> And every now and then she'll say: 'How do I spell such and such a word?' (21)

> He started playing a computer game called Rhunescape and that has this messaging thing on it so that you can type messages but he really did not want to spell words wrong so we spent about six months of him asking the spelling of everything that he was typing and he is now 14 and he is probably the most competent speller of all three of them. (26)

Both of them went through a year each of asking us how to spell things when they were bothered about spelling but they've long since stopped doing that. But they did when they first got into writing; they asked us how to spell things. (1)

Every day she'll come to me and say 'How do you spell this? How do you spell this? How do you write that?' She does not really like to make words up, she likes to know exactly how to spell it. Every day she does writing off her own bat and she's just picking it up. (24)

Children also seemed to acquire spellings by picking them up using strategies like phonetics, memory, comparison with other words and their own trial and error.

[She] likes to be read to and she can spell odd words as well. She can spell some basic words which is quite amazing which she just picks up from doing with [her sister]. … She'll say, how do you spell cat? c-a-t, so she's picked that up while she's sitting there eating breakfast or is behind us playing. (25)

And when she was writing 'happy' and I was spelling it out for her she said, 'I know there's double p in happy' so she knows some things although we haven't made a point of it. She knows by seeing us doing it and birthdays and Christmas. (17)

Some children, rather than asking, put considerable effort into working out their own spellings. In the following passage written by a six year-old girl it is possible to discern the use of phonetics as in 'cums', memory as in 'toyshop', combining of known spellings with invention to tackle an unknown word as in 'allwas', using known letter combinations in the midst of invention as in 'boorthdy'. It is also possible to discern where words are worked out again and again, with slightly different results each time, 'wundfol', 'wunbrol', a measure of the effort which goes into invented spelling where each word may be treated as a brand new task. The 'a's added to the ends of many of the words arose from saying these words out loud and with emphasis to attempt to discern the component sounds. Many consonants then have the auditory appearance of ending with an 'e' or an 'a' (for a facsimile see Appendix 2).

Sory
psDmoman cums and gives avryboody a Avtahcon to AnGlyna BoorThdy prty. All the nya fransa caThD up and sator to The prty. On The War the frans sdop of At A Toyshop and Bi A Beg prasont foor Anglyana. The frans sdop At The Bus sdop and wat Andtil A BiG rAD Bus cums cums up The Bus Bring Tham t the prty. The prty Goorla HASA A Vary BiG Haws.

Thea Giv The prasant to AngLyna Thac you sasa AnGLyna And unraps
The prasontAt insid The prity riping Thear is A DoLL's Haws 'iv Allwas
wonted A Doll's Hawsa. Thea'r HaWa a wundfol prty. And a wunbrol
Trep Bag. The EnD

Transcription: Postman comes and gives everybody an invitation to
Angelina's birthday party. All the nice friends dressed [?] up and set off
to the party. On the way the friends stop off at a toyshop and buy a big
present for Angelina. The friends stop at the bus stop and wait until a
big red bus comes up. The bus brings them to the party. The party girl
has a very big house. They give the present to Angelina. 'Thank you' says
Angelina and unwraps the present. Inside the pretty wrapping there is a
dolls' house, 'I've always wanted a dolls' house!' They have a wonderful
party. And a wonderful trip back. The End. (14)

Despite the large number of errors in this piece it can, nevertheless be viewed as
a step in the logical progression to competence. It is clear that this child knows
a good deal about writing although she has received no direct teaching. Words
are correctly distinguished with spaces between them and the spelling shows
serious efforts in the face of a lot of uncertainty to combine what she already
knows with phonetic attempts to work out words. An attempt has similarly
been made at punctuation showing that a lot has been picked up although its
use is, as yet, unrefined.

Glenda Bissex, recording her son Paul's writing development, also shows
his spelling moving gradually from his own worked-out inventions towards
conventionality. One of his first attempts at writing, interestingly, was a
message he badly wanted to convey to his mother who was preoccupied and
not paying attention to him. He wrote 'RUDF?' (Are you deaf?) Bissex charts
Paul's progress including his growing ability to use visual as well as auditory
clues and to take into account a wider range of possibilities in settling on the
spelling of a particular word. His ability, she argues, cannot be attributed to
either his work in school or the informal assistance that he received at home.
Instead she places a good deal of emphasis on Paul's own ability to work out
a particular spelling for himself. In this she sees her son as being typical rather
than remarkable in his achievements. The idea that children simply memorize
long lists of unpredictable words, she argues, does not explain the competences
of mature spellers and readers. These processes she then links to the cultivation
of a more general attitude towards learning; inventive spellers she says begin
from the belief that they can work things out for themselves. It is an attitude that
is likely to fit well with the philosophies of many home-educating families.

Working things out for yourself can of course lead off into very unpredictable
directions. One parent described their child's early grasp of spelling as being
purely visual and therefore virtually indecipherable. Yet by the age of 11 he
was writing to a high standard.

As a young child he had the most appalling spelling. As a six and seven year old he appeared to spell things, not phonetically but according to how he remembered the word to look. So he might have a word like 'huge' with letters that go above the line like h and ones that are below the line like g. But when he wrote it he'd have a b instead of an h or he'd have a y instead of a g or a p instead of a g – so he might have written 'buyo' instead of 'huge'. Phonetically it was nothing like the word he meant but when you looked at it, it was a similar shape to the right word.

[Now aged 11] We've done no work on spelling at all. He's just absorbed it by reading and gradually improved and now his spelling is very, very good. He writes well; he spells well; he knows where to put the quotation marks and exclamation marks. I think his writing is better than many adults but he hasn't been taught how to write he just knows from reading experience and from practice. (5)

One of the main ways in which spelling seemed to improve was simply a growing familiarity with the written word gained implicitly and incidentally through reading, which could lead to an informally acquired awareness of the conventions of spellings, such that words begin to look right or to look wrong. This type of improvement appears to be in no way unique. Many parents felt that spelling and punctuation had simply improved, with very little deliberate effort.

The following two examples show the difference which a year can make in writing competence. The first is a spontaneously written piece by a five year old, one of the first things she ever wrote without help, the second is the same piece dictated to her a year later. During this time no specific teaching had occurred but clearly a good deal of learning and familiarization with the written word had taken place.

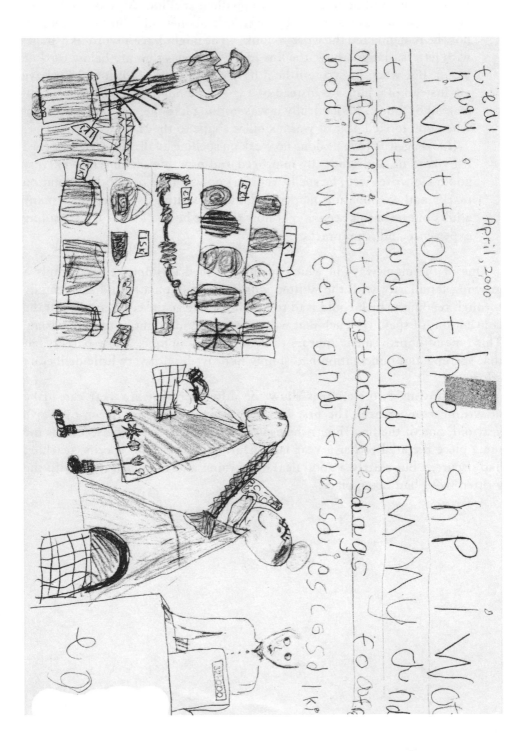

Facsimile of one child's writing at age five

27.2.2001

I went to the shop
I wontid to get
meada and Tom and
I for me. I wontid
to get ester eggs
for evr body and
the ester eggs
costid 1kd.

Facsimile of one child's writing the same material one year later, aged 6

Other parents described similar processes.

> We've done no work on spelling at all. He's just absorbed it by reading and gradually improved and now his spelling is very, very good. (5)

> He'd written something else, I've forgotten what it was, but I counted up on the list before he started asking us questions about spelling and I said well look this is what he's just written. There are 70 words on the page. I think 59 of them were spelt correctly and the others weren't. I said, considering he's never had a spelling test, he's never had any lessons in writing, he's never had any lessons, he's never had anyone tell him anything, I think that's pretty astonishing really. Surely, if he's going like this now, in two or three years I bet there will probably be something like 65 out of 70. (1)

Similar processes of simple familiarization may be at work with regard to areas like punctuation and grammar, perhaps supplemented with some self-directed requests for assistance or explanation. One parent saw a mixture of methods and strategies combining to create an easy going and enjoyable process in which writing as a whole, rather than spelling or grammar as separate issues, developed in its own time.

> [She's] got a pen pal in Boston and she writes emails to her and we go over the spelling before she sends them and I correct the spelling with her so that she knows which is the right way. She might have written something down that sounds right but is actually spelt wrong. She's had a good bash at it. But it's coming along. It's just that we don't do it religiously every day. Maybe it's a bit slower than it would be at school. But I think that by the time they come to be adults their spelling will be fine. I'd much rather they develop their mental independence and be able to problem solve and what have you than that the spelling is perfect at this age ... [She's] into puzzle books. Quite often, every night, I see her with her puzzle book, she's doing various crosswords, number puzzles and all sorts of things so she's writing in letters here and there, words and what have you. But it's not essay writing, anything like that. So probably their written punctuation needs work. But that's just something that needs a bit of practice. The thoughts are there. The creative thinking is there. (6)

Handwriting

Handwriting is a perceptuo-motor skill that can only be practised by doing it unlike other aspects of writing such as narrative, expression and so on that can be improved through interaction with language, written and spoken and without much actual writing. For this reason and perhaps because the use of computers and word processing were very popular the standard of actual handwriting was often not up to that expected in school.

> Their handwriting is fairly atrocious. (21)

> He kept a diary until very recently and his cousin laughed at him because his writing was so poor. He was 11 or 12 then and it stopped him for about six months and then he did it again and he worked on his handwriting to make it neat. (1)

Despite this, parents did not seem to be anxious about handwriting and some questioned its relevance, outside schools, in the modern world.

> My writing is pretty illegible and so is [my partner's] actually. I went through years of schooling so I should write perfectly. I can read it but if I'm writing in a hurry even I have trouble some of the time. Other people can't read it. The value of writing is becoming less and less with computers so it's not necessarily a skill that is useful to her in any real sense. She should be able to fill out forms and things like this but in many respects she's never going to use [hand] writing that much. (6)

> Others held the attitude that poor handwriting would not take long to improve if and when the need should arise.

> I don't really care about it because I think at some point if it bothers him he's going to change it and it won't take him very long. (1)

One family showed how this point had been reached and handwriting difficulties had been overcome.

> Both of them, coming up to the English exam, they did do some just sitting and writing to get their writing speed and strength up a bit and the essays that they had done for English they typed all the ones that they could because they are very competent on the computer but they needed just the physical act of handwriting they needed to get that up to speed ... But it didn't seem to be a problem and [she] got an A on the English and [her sister] got a B at GCSE despite the fact that she is very dyslexic ... They saw that there might be a slight issue and they addressed it, but again it didn't need ten years of writing in school to get their writing good enough. (26)

Developing writing

As with reading, it soon became apparent that no two children followed exactly the same route to writing competence. Different individuals saw different things in writing and reacted in different ways to the possibilities and challenges that it offered. For many, the purposes for which they needed or wanted to use writing offered sufficient practice for competence to gradually grow.

> I was watching [him] writing on the computer, he can write quite mature expressions in sentence form, he's not writing just garbage even when he's just chatting to the people that he's playing an online game with ... they don't do it that often but nevertheless they can express themselves very clearly in writing and they like playing with writing. [She] has been writing stories with a very peculiar, whimsical sort of style and she loves doing it. (21)

> And another huge thing in our family has been Dungeons and Dragons and it involves everybody, even me to some extent and that's made him write. You have to write information down, you have to make these charts. (16)

> Well, I remember him sitting there getting faster and faster at typing and just being amazed watching him learn without doing anything at all, just maybe telling him how to spell one or two things but he picked that up from other people. He'll remember spellings ...[he wanted] to learn to play the game, not to learn to spell or write. (21)

> It's practice from a self-motivated point of view. Rather than having a teacher say, 'You need to practise these to develop automatic response' or something like that, it is the child thinking, 'I want to be able to write like Mum and Dad so ...' and then they practise. (5)

For others there were more dramatic turning points.

> Writing and stuff she hates and I haven't ever pursued that, or spelling. She's one of these children who puts their hands over their ears, always has done since she was a baby. If she doesn't want to know anything her hands go over her ears. None of my kids liked formal lessons or formal instruction at all and as soon as you start on telling them how words are spelt: 'I don't want to hear that. I just want you to tell me how to spell rainbow.' [And yet] the other day we walked through the local bookshop. They asked her if she would like to review books for them, children's books. She was thrilled with this. She has to write a 60 word review. So

she brought the book home and read it and wrote the 60 word review. How do you spell this and that. They use the reviews for the monthly newsletter for the children's club. She wrote a 100 word review and had to take it down to 60 which she did herself.

The boys were like that too. They never liked spelling. They both hated writing with a passion. It wasn't until [one of them] was 15 and decided to go to Melbourne Uni. to get a degree. He went to [someone who had been an English teacher] and said 'Teach me how to write an essay.' It took him about a year. He went to her every time he had to write one, on a needs basis. And that's how they've all learned, on a needs basis. (7)

This mother described how her son, aged 13, saw the need to improve his English, which he did, when he began to follow up his interests in maths and computing at adult education classes.

The choice was his again but we went along to the orientation day and he did an assessment and they said his maths skills were pretty good and so he signed up for computers and then the next semester he signed up for maths which were the two he wanted to do and he also did – this is a very interesting thing actually – an English assessment as well and at this point his written English skills were quite poor. He'd only been reading for a couple of years, two and a half to three years at that point and he had done very little writing at all. He'd done a fair bit of typing because of the requirements for what he was doing on the computer. And computers are quite unforgiving about spelling errors on the words you use in computer programs. So you have to spell the words in your program exactly right or the computer won't understand it. It meant his knowledge of spelling was really quite specialized. [Overall] his spelling at that point was so poor that he couldn't read it back himself when he wrote stuff down. And he was sort of aware of this and I was very aware of it but I felt that he didn't have enough confidence in himself to be put in a position where that was tested. And I asked him not to do the English assessment and he said: 'No, no, no, I want to try it.' And he did the English one as well and he realized in himself how completely bad it was, mostly because it was illegible and he couldn't read it back. They marked it and they said they didn't think he could do the English unit at Grade 10 level [GCSE] because he was not up to it. 'But we do have a literacy class that we put adults into who need some help to get up to that standard.' And I was sitting there – I was trying to let him be the person in the interview when they were talking to him. And he said to them: 'Yes I'd like to do that.' And this was out of the blue. This is from a child who refused to write anything for 12 years and can't spell 'the' and the last thing I wanted to do was pressure him into it because I felt there had been no indication from him that he felt good enough about it to have it out there in public. He just went and did it and joined this literacy class. They said to him: 'You can do this class for six weeks or six years. It doesn't matter. Do it as long as you want and then when you are ready to go up to the Grade 10 standard then you can do that.' The very first lesson they actually are going through the alphabet with them. This is for illiterate adults. And then the second lesson they are talking about vowels and consonants and what's the difference between them. And six months later he was in the Grade 10 class. He actually completed that with very little input from me. I reminded him occasionally if he had an assignment due but other than that I stayed out of it and it was him who did it and his spelling in that time just improved out of sight. You wouldn't believe it. It was something ready to happen in his mind, suddenly clicked and started making sense. And now, of course, he's 15 and he's discovering that girls chat to each other and modern-day girls chat to each other via email and to do that you've got to write. (3)

For some, writing became a passion; something that they found their own enjoyment in and which they pursued for its own sake. We were able to see some examples of writing from the 14 year old in the next quote. These were of a very high standard, certainly of educated adult level in relation to both narrative and description and technically faultless.

[He] has a stack of writing that he's done. He's produced a prodigious amount of fiction in books using the computer. I think it comes about from his voracious reading. There's been no conscious effort to teach him how to put a story together or how to develop characters or plot other than I read what he writes and I comment on it and say, 'I like the way you've done this. Maybe if you did that …' We don't sit down and say: Now, this is how you write a story. You've got to write the introduction and so on. It's just that he's read so much and he knows the elements of a story though he may not know the names for them. (5)

Others clearly found a similar enjoyment.

[She] spends a lot of her spare time reading or writing. There's a list that she's joined called the Silver Mountain – it's a website on the subject of wolves and you have characters that you write about and you have to be extremely literate or the site does not accept your post, it has to be over a certain length and you are writing about your wolf's character. And it's built up huge stories and F has to use words and spell checks, because it has to be very literate to get past the moderators of the list and she sends a lot of her writing there. (20)

She's always liked words and she loves reading and she loves writing. She's always written everything from birthday cards to notes for herself, notes for me, letters to people, stories, half-finished plays. She likes writing. It's something that she always thinks she's good at. (3)

He got interested in writing stories and he does write huge stories on the computer. (21)

He actually wrote twelve pages of a novel at one point; he actually started writing a book and he read it out loud to an audience at a literary reading when he was ten, with fantastic self-confidence … [My partner] was worried about him and he came up with this. (1)

As with reading, children clearly took different routes to writing proficiency. The common thread is that, without the years of deliberate teaching given in school they all reached a level of competence sufficient for practical purposes and some went much further than this. How has this been achieved? It seems that writing is a good example of how incidental learning can work. Without having to do very much writing itself there were several ways to gain knowledge about it through other pursuits. Indeed, with the exception of actual handwriting, the skills which contribute to spelling, grammar, understanding of genre, writing conventions and creativity can all be enhanced without much actual writing taking place. First there is exposure to the written word through a wide variety of literature read aloud to them by their parents, listened to on tapes and, as they gain in competence, what they read for themselves. As well, there is day-to-day contact with the various kinds of written material that are found in everyday life. Secondly, through play children have the opportunity to practise creating their own narratives and characters. Thirdly there is the opportunity at home to develop oracy. Children have countless and extended opportunities in the course of conversation to develop writing genres indirectly, such as narrative, explanation, description, logical argument etc. without putting pen to paper. Some children do write from an early age and bring this knowledge to bear on their work. In these cases they are able to concentrate on the aspects of writing they find most important at the time. There is no pressure to achieve technical accuracy, so they are able to focus solely on content if they so wish. Other children avoid writing for a long time, only turning their attention to it when they perceive a practical need to do so: writing letters or emails, to join an online group, or when they embark on formal study. Whichever way children choose to develop their writing it is the incidental and unquantifiable input over a long period of time that appears crucial. The knowledge gained in this way can then be put to use when required, whether for enjoyment or practical purpose.

Chapter 10

Numeracy

Along with literacy, maths forms the backbone of the primary school curriculum and, as with literacy, there has been considerable and ongoing debate as to how it should be taught. Whatever competing methods there are, maths is generally perceived to be a subject that is highly and logically structured. Formal educational approaches tend to deal in terms of 'mastering basics' and 'crucial building blocks'. A glance at the national maths curriculum illustrates how children are expected to develop understanding. Knowledge is projected to grow in a linear progression. Children begin with adding and subtracting and then move on to multiplying and dividing. Whole numbers are mastered first, then work begins on fractions and decimals. Other aspects of basic maths: number patterns, various forms of measurement, tables, graphs, simple statistics, transport timetables, problem solving and so on are also fed into the curriculum. Whatever is being taught, great care is taken to present the material in carefully graded steps, clearly visible in the progress displayed in written exercises. The chaotic nature of informal learning, with very little written down, stands in stark contrast. Added to this, maths is also a subject which, perhaps more than any other, induces some degree of fear, especially for those parents who might feel their own knowledge to be inadequate.

> I view myself as pretty much a maths dunce. One of my main concerns with having the children at home beyond primary school was, because I was in a remedial maths group in Form One in High School. And I'm thinking how can I possibly help to support these children when I can't even do it. (2)

These two factors combined lead many parents to treat maths rather differently to other subjects. Griffith (1998) for example notes that informal US home-educating parents often opt for a 'we unschool everything except math' approach. The parents in this study did, for the most part, retain an informal approach in relation to numeracy though a few did express some concerns.

It is a worry that we have that there isn't enough maths going on. (4)

… though the following parent found that her anxiety was unfounded.

> One of my panic attacks this year was Kevin and his maths. I thought, 'He's 14. I'd better make sure he's covered everything he should have.' So we actually ordered a maths book. I explained to [him], 'I just want to make sure we are not neglecting anything. So if you can just work your way through this book gradually and make sure you've covered all of Year 8 maths I'll be happy.' He did the first four pages and got 95% correct. Then he said, 'Mum, it's dead boring.' So we gave up on that idea. Instead we picked up a student handbook from a second-hand shop. So we opened that at the maths section and spent about an hour going through, saying ok, here's the addition and subtraction content, went through that – yes – understand that bit, division and multiplication – yes – understand that, percentages, no worries. So we worked our way through, not teaching, just checking, for my benefit that he understood the mathematical concepts. He did. (5)

In his earlier study (see Chapter 2) Thomas (1998), using one mother's extremely detailed diaries, traced the everyday informal acquisition of primary level numeracy for a single child. Interestingly, this showed a very non-linear progression. Opportunistic learning such as adding in 20s preceded lower denomination multiplication because the former had a practical application when collecting the 20 cent deposits from shopping trolleys left abandoned in supermarket car parks. A marked feature was the inexplicable advances and regressions she made. In this chapter we take a broader look at the informal acquisition of maths.

Learning maths from everyday life

There is little doubt that all children learn a great deal of maths informally for themselves before being taught in school. Nunes and Bryant (quoted in Wood, 1998) have researched children learning maths both in and out of school and attest to the widespread nature of such learning.

> Take any mathematical concept taught in primary school, and you will find that children have some understanding of this concept before they are taught about it formally. (Nunes and Bryant, quoted in Wood, 1998: 265)

To us, there seems no reason to assume that such knowledge cannot continue to develop informally. Once again, we found that the informal curriculum is an excellent provider of maths learning opportunities. Far from being a subject detached from everyday life as it is often treated, maths, like the written word, is all around us, and numeracy skills are in daily use. Moreover, most of the primary curriculum if not more, can be covered in this way: telling the time, counting money, making a paper house, colouring patterns, sharing food, weighing cooking ingredients, working out how many days to a birthday, estimating how long a car journey will take, laying the table, playing board games. Many mathematical concepts arise spontaneously and attract child interest; the list above contains just a selection of the myriad of possiblities and parents gave some more.

> People tend to think of maths as divorced from everyday life, but it's not really because there's a lot of maths in everyday life. There's numbers, fractions and measurement in cooking. There's numbers on clocks and videos. Children are very motivated to work out how the video recorder works. There's programming the microwave and all those things. Then there's money – adding their pocket money, taking away what they have spent. There's maths in shopping – both at the supermarket and for things they really want. They might have some birthday money to spend and we notice that Lego is on sale at 20% off so they work out which sets they can afford with the money they have. Then there is the stuff they pick up just through conversation – the names of shapes and three-dimensional shapes and so on. Almost all of primary school maths is covered without any effort at all. (5)

> Um, you mean adding and subtraction? Yeah. Well the answer to that is that because you need it to play Monopoly and to buy sweets from a shop and you are going along in a car and you say those three sheep, they are weird, or whatever … As I said, I suppose very quickly they get the idea of, I mean money is what does it I think. You have a certain amount of pocket money. You have certain things you want to buy with it, whether that's sweets or comics or whatever, that teaches you incredibly quickly subtraction and addition. And there are probably quite a lot of other things … (1)

> [It's] the kind of maths that you and I use every day, like if I'm making a pizza dough and it's a recipe for one dough and I need to triple it … it takes 2⅔ cups of flour [for one pizza], how much do I need for a triple recipe? It's very easy for them to picture that in their minds and give me the answer. Or, you know, we built a skating rink out the back and I needed to know how much wood I needed. We measure the length and calculate it. (8)

As with reading and writing parents are role models who demonstrate, through their own activities, the importance and uses of maths in everyday life. Parents cook, shop, schedule outings, check money in purse or pocket, talk about mortgages and bills, the time left before having to leave the house and so on. Children are able to pick up bits and pieces from this stream of information of which maths is an integral part. Parents also talk to children about topics with mathematical content, although the aim of the conversation may be something entirely different. They sing nursery rhymes, count how many people are in front in the post office queue, talk about why there are numbers on buses, calculate the cost of a holiday or a household item, measure how much a child has grown since last year, compare ages with other children, discuss speed and distance in the car, prices and discounts in the shops and so on. Again, in parallel with literacy, children are surrounded by common household objects with mathematical content. These might commonly include clocks, transport timetables, weighing scales, rulers, the speedometer in the car, calculators and so on. More child-centred resources include puzzles, construction kits, books, games, building bricks and craft materials. Some of these may have been provided with the direct intention of stimulating interest in numbers, some because they were interesting or worthwhile in other ways and the maths potential was simply incidental to this. One parent described how she provided maths resources that tied in with her son's interest in knights. This was obviously intended to engage his attention but was presented without any element of compulsion.

> We've got quite a few books with a mathematical flavour. Partly that's me trying to make sure there is some maths in their reading diet. For example, I bought a series of books for [him] called *Sir Cumference*. They are picture books about a knight called Sir Cumference and his son Radius and his wife called Lady Di Ameter and they have adventures. And because they are knights they are interesting for [him] and he gets the mathematical concepts at the same time as the story. So there are things like that where I make a conscious effort to incorporate mathematical learning in a way which will be attractive. But often there are times when I make a positive attempt to introduce something like that and if it's not popular then ok, it sits on the shelf and no one ever looks at it. But if it is popular, that's good. (5)

Once again, parents followed up children's own interests and questions. This is not a teacher deciding what to teach, but children asking for assistance in their own learning. There is no lesson introduction and explanation, no adult-directed questions, no exercises.

> Both reading and maths, we would have given them lessons if they'd wanted it, but that's all, just given them the method and let them get on

with it ... the other day actually M couldn't understand, I'm not sure what exactly, but something about fractions so I went right back to the beginning, got a piece of paper and folded it up and just wrote down what a half looks like, what a quarter looks like, folding this piece of paper and she said, 'that's great, I understand that' so I left the piece of paper hanging on the wall. So as far as that's concerned it's just when they come up with a question, we'll teach them a bit if they want it. (21)

Parents naturally take the opportunity to involve their children in anything that they themselves are enthusiastic about. This father obviously inspired an interest in maths and 'drummed' some into his daughters when they were very young. He obviously takes pleasure in explaining any aspect of maths on request, in this case what algebra is about. But the children's interest remains a critical factor – these are the girls who rebelled when asked to write less than ten words a day in their diaries.

... And the other thing, you talk about your own enthusiasms as a parent. I kind of like numbers. I think they are neat and like the interrelationships of them and things like that, so we have had charts up which highlight the prime numbers or is a multiplication table and things like that. But [nothing else] except for a brief jab for [the younger one] four years ago when she said, 'Give me some maths problems' and I wrote a program to print out lots of sums, you know, 30 on the page and she would work through them and ask me to tick the ones that were correct and that kind of thing, so that lasted a couple of weeks ...

Just last week [my older daughter] read a book about Richard Feynman, the Nobel physicist. It's full of funny stories and so it's a good read. But in one of them he was talking about elementary algebra and he was saying there's this formula so [she] said, 'What's algebra?' and I think I covered [much of what algebra is about] in about 10 minutes. And that will be enough for her not to be phased if she needs algebra in the next five years anyway. She'll be able to go from there and say yes, algebra, I know that ... She has the essence of it now. ... I tried to drum into her head, about four years ago, the pairs of numbers which add up to 10, like 3 and 7 and 4 and 6 – that's very important for all your bigger additions, if you have those pat then most mental and written arithmetic is dead easy. And knowing what the square numbers are, so they know that 7 squared is one-less-than-50, that's a kind of mantra for them. So they are getting a good feel for numbers ... (4)

Overall, however, parents referred almost exclusively to learning incidents or opportunities which arose spontaneously. In other words the lack of any preset structure in their maths input did not appear to constitute an obstacle to learning it informally.

Children's own activities

As with reading and writing, as soon as children had a modicum of competence they began to put this to use in their own lives. One of the main inspirations for doing 'sums' was money, either pocket money or earned money.

> *Child*: At Christmas the three of us put our money in together and then made a list of what we wanted to buy with the prices. We didn't have nearly enough and had to scale the whole thing down. (14)

I think that 'dumbing down' adult life for children in order to teach them the skills they need for adult life is just pointless. You just treat them as adults as much as they are capable of being. My kids have had bank accounts for years. They've had online access to their bank accounts. My eight year old logs on and transfers 15 cents to his brother's account because his brother bought him an ice cream and he only had 60 cents and he borrowed the other 15 cents because he needed 75 cents. This is the kind of thing they just do because they are capable of doing that. I'm not going to give them pocket money or play money or something to learn about money. I'm going to give them a bank account and make them earn some money. I've never given them pocket money. Every bit of money my kids get they've earned. So my eleven year old has a paper run and my eight year old and my ten year old do a quarter of that paper run and every month they set up an automatic transfer which goes from my eleven year old's account into the other two accounts. He actually pays them a reduced rate because he's the one who's responsible for carrying the papers up to the house and folding them and they just have to do the delivery. But they earn $3.50 a month and then they can choose how to spend that. So, if your objective is to teach children enough maths so that they are financially competent then you treat them as financially competent people and help them to learn anything they need to learn. (3)

Virtually any craft or construction activity will involve some element of maths such as measuring, estimating, considering angles, counting, symmetry, pattern making, geometry etc. These activities may also provide some less obvious opportunities for using practical maths.

> *Child*: When I am beading I always count the beads in threes, because it is quicker and easier. (14)

Children's games often have some mathematical dimension to them in terms of counting, computation, logic, probability etc. Obvious examples are board, card and computer games.

With Dungeons and Dragons they have dice; they have to work out all sorts of arithmetic things to play the game. (16)

Another thing that he's done from computer games is percentages, percentage marks on a particular game for example, he understands that really well. From that he knows that 50% is half and so on. (15)

Other kinds of games provide different types of opportunity, perhaps planning an imaginary journey, playing shop or, as in this case, playing trains.

Mother: A lot of learning happens in play. The boys spend hours and hours playing – sometimes a game goes all day; some games are so long that the boys play what they call 'episodes' of them – so the game is a regular one that they pick up again the next day or the next week and continue from where they were up to. They might have a game set up and it could be a game of trains on the floor and the conversation might be about what time the train's going to leave this station and arrive at that station and how many kilometres away it is and it should take longer to get from here to there because that's a longer track. So a certain amount of mathematical knowledge is just picked up in play conversation.
Son (aged 14): Not necessarily. The train [on the longer track] could be going faster. (5)

Most children love to play with construction kits. How much mathematical knowledge is derived from this activity is difficult to ascertain but there is little doubt that the potential is there for the development of spatial and technological understanding.

At the moment he's in a very physical, practical phase. He spends all his time building and designing K'nex and Lego and this kind of thing, construction toys. And he's actually really good. He can follow a diagram; you know, take it from a 2D diagram and make it into a 3D thing. And some of them are really complicated and you have to look carefully to see which bit goes with which bit and he does that really well ... he's building construction toys all the time, constantly. And he just designs things now. He used to start off doing everything from the diagrams and put them together. We got his first construction things when he was five, so he's been doing it for two years now. Now he can just design things in his head and put them together. I've done things with him, with the diagrams. I find that quite, quite challenging, some of them, aimed at ten year olds, some of the stuff he's got. It's actually quite hard sometimes to see where they go; transpose it from a 2D to a 3D image. ... now he just designs things out of his head and puts them together. (6)

As with reading and writing children found that maths was a tool which could be used to further other hobbies and to extend their knowledge in areas that had come to interest them.

> *Mother*: [She is] learning a huge amount through cooking at the moment. She's adjusting recipes ...
> *Daughter* (aged 13): I got one, one day when I was going on a [web]site. It was an American site so everything was in cups, so that day I learnt all the conversions through cups to ounces to grams and back again through all of them, fluid ounces into grams. (6)

> Once, [his Dad said to him] 'Look, help me. I need 11 spadefuls of sand.' [He] went off, came back after a while and said: 'When you said you wanted me to help you, is it 5½ each?' Again, he was working with real stuff. They take what is at the right level for them. It's the same with making a cake and measuring things. It's not like working in the physical world according to a curriculum, but with intelligent purpose. It's genuine real-world value. In this way of doing things you can't make a mistake. It's real. If you get the cake mix wrong you have to throw it away ...
> Once we were tiling the bathroom and we had tiles a foot square, a foot by 6 inches and 6 inches square. [He]was sitting there saying 'there's two of these in one of those'. He was just interacting with the physical reality. (13)

> [He] wanted to know how far it was to the moon and he looked in a book and he found how long it takes to travel to the moon, or how long it took in the days of the Apollo programme. He said 'Well if you know how fast the rocket's going, we could just multiply that by how long it takes and then we'll know.' I think if that had been a math problem in a book it would have stumped him or he would have felt like it would have stumped him ... They are continually measuring things. He has a hedgehog as a pet and he weighs her every week to see how much she weighs to make sure her weight is stable. We rescued a little baby mouse and we weigh him regularly first to see how much he's growing and then to see if his weight is stable, so we know how much food to give him. (8)

Note that nearly all these calculations are embedded in practical realities of what children actually want to do or need to do. They are not sums on paper which, once dealt with, are of no further consequence. They have, as one parent remarked, intelligent purpose.

Sometimes children simply picked up concepts or skills unbeknown to their parents and without apparent effort.

... At other times they just come up with things and I think 'Gee! He understands those percentages. I haven't actually told him about them. I don't know where he got that from.' (5)

[His] mental arithmetic is very good, much better than mine ... and that just happened, he hasn't been taught. (21)

Of course it is true that some children in school enjoy maths for its own sake as did some of ours who spontaneously practised mathematical procedures just for the fun of it.

They would have played some number games between themselves and with us, not again with any pedagogical content. I do remember them counting up to as far as they could count up to because they wanted to see how far they could count. And lying in bed and saying: Hey! I've got up to a hundred. And then saying ok and both saying ok, let's see if we can get any further. This was when they were four or five and seeing how far they could get. I know they played adding and subtracting games like that which were not anything to do with me and [my partner] but were just with finding out about numbers and seeing where they went. (1)

Child: I always do adding – I do sums, I pick a number like 6 say and add it up say 5 times. I give myself a problem like a baby has to be baby sat for 4 hours at £5 an hour and then that would be £20. That one's quite easy, sometimes I do harder ones. I used to do them when I was swimming my lengths but now I do them anywhere. (14)

He came in one day from jumping on the trampoline where he had been for some time. He told me that he had discovered that 1/3 is 2/3 of 1/2, that 1/4 is 3/4 of 1/3 and that 9/10 of 8/9 of 7/8 of 6/7 of 10 equals 6. (5)

We played a game of 'combination locks'. Someone writes down a four digit number and keeps it hidden, then you give the player some clues that refer to the digits as a, b, c and d. So you might have $a + b = 7$, $d + a = 6$, $c + 3 = 4$, $a + b + c + d = 10$ and then the player works out the hidden number. We played it for days. He just kept saying, 'give me another one'. (14)

Scaling up

As children get older the kind of maths that they need to do is scaled up in connection with why they need to do it. These mothers describe exactly this process in their children's lives and link growing mathematical competence with life aspirations and general maturation.

When [she] was ten she paid for a two week trip interstate, down to Melbourne in Victoria where my mother lives because she wanted to go on a holiday and she wanted to do it without her family and she wanted to visit her grandmother and she discovered that the ticket was only $100 each way and she could buy one on the internet. So, over a period of 10 months she saved up $200 and bought herself a return plane ticket and she went to Melbourne for two weeks. She's going to America at the end of this year. Things scale up as they get older ... So functional mathematics just comes from being a functional person. (3)

We've got a friend whose birthday was last Saturday. [She] was having a big party and they asked would she do some cooking for them. ... They said to [her] would she like to cook because she's eaten some of the stuff she's made here and it was really nice. So she did the lion's share of the cooking. She cooked several cakes, cooked some savoury stuff as well. What she had to do, she had to do it on a Friday because we are out all day Saturday and she actually came and picked it up Saturday morning. [She] had to plan because one of our ovens had stopped working. We've got a double oven and one doesn't work. She had to plan when to do it, when to get it into the oven because we had to leave here at quarter to four on Friday, so everything had to be cooked and ready all by then. So she had to plan ... so she got the whole planning experience as well as measuring things out and what have you, putting ingredients together. She had to structure how to do it so that everything was done in time. And it was all done in time. I helped. I was her assistant, that kind of thing, did all the donkey work. But she put all the things together and made everything and it was quite complicated. We had to sit and think, well this is going to take how long to cook and when it comes out we have to put this in, and this one has to be done while that one is cooking and there's a third thing to go in after that. And we had to change temperatures and everything else. It was quite an interesting experience for her. How to work under pressure without falling to pieces for a start and getting everything done. Her cakes went down very well. Everyone said they were lovely. (6)

Mathematics is a daily activity; counting money when we were volunteering at a thrift store. [The two of them] were at the till, counting money. They would often calculate the change before the cash register. It just knocked people over. They just couldn't believe it, but for them it's not very hard to count up from $1.75 to $2. They are not actually setting up a mathematical problem in their head and subtracting. They are looking at it from a very practical perspective. (8)

For many however, the question remains of how far informal learning of maths can actually go. There are certain areas of abstract maths which simply seem very unlikely to crop up on a day-to-day basis. For some though, this was a non-problem.

> We haven't found that point yet [when informal learning runs out]. With algebra it's still natural learning. If they ask why is the sky blue we just say, 'Well let's find out.' If they ask, 'What is algebra, anyway?' It's the same. ... He's done some algebra too, not flogged through an exercise book. He has just picked up a book, had a read and said, 'Oh that's how it works.' And his reading has covered those sorts of things too, with books like *The Number Devil* ... Again this is somewhere where I am not always aware of what the children know. I'm really pleased when they read a book about maths and think they will be learning whilst they are reading and then I find out later that they already knew and understood the mathematical content but just enjoyed the book anyway ... (5)

Teachers might argue that apparently leaving maths to chance could mean that a lot of what is taught in school is missed, leaving children at a disadvantage if they turned to formal learning at a later stage in school or college. However, it does not appear that the years of relying on informal learning left the children disadvantaged. Those who developed a mathematical interest either in its own right or to support some other purpose were able to pursue it in the same way that they would any other hobby. This mother describes how her son followed up the maths relevant to his interest in 3D graphics.

> I have found that the kids who need to know algebra and trigonometry and differential calculus which is my son because you need a lot of that stuff, especially for 3D graphics, you need a lot of geometry, a lot of trig., a lot of that kind of stuff – you teach it to them. You sit down and go: 'Ah, how do I work out what the length of the triangle is if all I know is this and this angle?' If I didn't know I'd look it up or I'd find someone who could teach it to him. I happen to know the answer to that question. I taught it to him; it took ten minutes. It's not a big deal for kids who are confident in their abilities, who are motivated to learn it and those who have the resources available to find out that information. (3)

Interests such as these can lead right the way into courses involving university level maths and beyond. This young man is currently completing a PhD in aeronautical engineering.

> Computers had started to come in by the time he was 13. It wasn't a big thing early on but he fell in love with computers. He started designing his own model yachts. He learned computer programs to do it, design

the yacht and then go and sail it which totally blew me away because I didn't understand anything of what he was doing. He's got a whole heap of things he designed when he was 12 or 13. And he thought nothing of it. And neither did I really until I looked back. He loved it. He spent all his time on that ... Then aircraft started coming into that and he started making model planes. He still does. He's got a huge workshop where he's making helicopters. [At 15] we moved back down to Melbourne. Again, I didn't know what he was after. A lot of it, rockets, he started to make model rockets ... rocket science. He started to become really interested. But I don't think at that stage that he even realized he could do anything professionally like that. It was, like way up here – he thought it would be way above him. (7)

Alternatively, some children felt the external pressures to be mathematically competent in the school sense and decided for themselves to study the subject systematically for the sake of future study and career prospects.

Daughter (aged 13): I do a little bit [of maths] most days. It's a self-teaching book that I'm doing at the moment. I usually do a few pages or I might get into a whole chapter or I might read another chapter again. And some days I won't do anything. ... I'm doing it because I think that mathematics is actually a basic skill that, in Western society, you need for later life, for career, for university if I want to go there, for anything. ... I've found since I was quite young ... I've found maths fun. Like some people like jigsaw puzzles. When I was younger I did it because it was fun. I do it now partly because I recognize that it's something that I do need, that I'm going to need for the rest of my life. It's just a skill that you need to practise. (6)

Or this girl who decided to enrol in Grade 11...

At 15 she decided next year was Grade 11 [first year of college]. We were horrified but tried to be relaxed about it. Her plan was to do an adult ed. course for 18 weeks, to get up to Grade 10 level in maths. We shook our heads, remembering how she'd been [so negative about maths] but we took her. She got a High Achievement. She really worked hard to get it. (11)

The amount of maths that children did varied enormously. Some pursued it right the way up to career level whilst others probably did not get beyond a basic understanding. In keeping with our thesis that children will imbibe the culture around them, they all seem to achieve or be well on the way to achieving functional maths – the level of mathematical ability which adults need in their day-to-day lives. If they are interested they will take it further. This is the comment from a parent in a family where one child had pursued maths far beyond his age level and was admitted to a course in Further Education to further maths together with computing. His younger sister was different; not seeing the relevance of maths beyond the everyday level.

> If I tried to sit down to teach her sines and working out things she wouldn't care. It's got nothing to do with her life at the moment. She doesn't want to learn it. She'd be doing it on sufferance because I was requiring it of her. And even if I managed to get her to regurgitate the information, six months down the track she's not going to remember what it was. So why should I bother? (3)

The most striking aspect of children learning maths informally is the practical nature of it. The children did not see maths in the conventional sense, as an activity undertaken with little relation to real life. Rather, they encountered maths, as they did reading and writing, as a means of getting things done; as a practical step in achieving something else. One consequence of this is that errors have real-life consequences – divide the cake wrongly and not everyone will get a piece. The chances to spot errors and to self-correct are therefore fairly high.

Another feature of basic maths is that things that people do with numbers in real life, add them up, divide them, take them away from other numbers and so on are performed largely as mental operations, not written ones. In fact, writing down calculations might even hamper understanding. As Carraher *et al.* (1985) point out, both the conventions and abstraction of early written maths may constitute a barrier to working out calculations. We can speculate that the practical approach, combining low levels of abstraction and freedom of method are strengths of informal learning at least basic numeracy informally.

Although parents barely touched on it, thereby suggesting that in their eyes at least, there was no difficulty, children at some stage were able to transfer from this practical base to more abstract levels of maths. For some, like the girl last mentioned, it appears that maths remains essentially a practical tool. For many being able to competently handle numbers at the day-to-day level is enough. For others, interest pushes them into the further reaches of mathematical knowledge whether out of intrinsic interest or because they feel they ought to. In either case the informal learning was found to have provided a solid base for further study.

Chapter 11

Towards a deeper understanding of informal learning

We began this research with a question: How do children learn informally at home? More specifically, how do those, whose learning is informal, acquire an education on a par with that provided by schools but with very little, if any, of the structure associated with learning in school? On the face of it, the proposition that informal learning within the family can replace formal learning in school is a remarkable one: that without a set curriculum, planned teaching, structured lessons, regular assessment, age-related targets or even clear goals, children may learn from life at home what school, with all its professional expertise, seeks to impart.

We already know that children learn a tremendous amount informally in early childhood, simply by being at home, engaging with their surroundings and the people, things and experiences that make up their normal everyday world. As a society we simply expect pre-school children to learn successfully from everyday life. When they begin school the assumption is that the learning then required of them, by virtue of its presumed deeper intellectual content, will need to be specifically arranged and presented; in short they will need to be deliberately taught. However, there seems to be no substance behind the idea that the efficacy of informal learning should run out at or around this point. Informal home education illustrates that it is quite feasible for children to continue learning in the same ways as before.

Two things in particular stand out through this study of informal learning; firstly the strength of children as autonomous learners in control not only of how and what they learn but also exerting considerable influence over the type and amount of assistance they require. Secondly, the way in which informal learning blends, and often disappears, into the rest of life. There is little in the way of current theory which can encompass either of these two aspects. Neo-Vygotskian theories assume that informal learning is teacher or parent directed with little room for child-initiated learning of the kind that permeates the pages of this book. Theories of adult informal learning are much more in lne with what we have described through the contacts used. But these are higher-order abstractions which do not explain the subject matter and manner of learning as it takes place during the nitty-gritty of children's day-to-day lives. This is precisely the place in which a new take on informal learning needs to be grounded. If we begin with a child's eye view of the learning situation, asking what attracts children's attention, why, and how they then go about exploring these things, we begin to be able to see learning as a form of growth in which children add, flexibly and organically, to their understanding of the world around them. Such a view further enables us to see how learning is structured by the child's day-to-day environment and is accomplished as an ongoing facet of the things that children do.

We have proposed three basic elements to the type of learning on which informal home education is based: what is learnt, how it is learnt, and the part played by parents.

First, the culture that surrounds children provides what we have called their informal curriculum. Everyday objects, other people and commonplace experiences provide children with a wealth of information on all manner of subjects, including the primary education mainstays of literacy and numeracy. Children are exposed to real-life skills such as shopping, using the telephone, cooking, money calculations, reading, travelling, dealing with people outside the family and so on. These skills are presented holistically, in the situations in which they are actually put to use. The broadening out of the cultural curriculum beyond the immediate and everyday takes place in many ways including conversation, children's own curiosity and investigations, often in the form of play, and the seeing and hearing of snippets of specialized knowledge from a variety of sources including the mass media, visits to museums and other places of interest, books and other people. As children develop they are free to follow up in more deliberate fashion the subjects which hold particular attraction for them by making use of conventional research techniques such as reading, using the internet, joining interest groups, seeking out other specialized sources of information, and of course, thinking out things for themselves.

Second, if the subject matter is there for children in the form of the informal curriculum, they still have to somehow engage with it. There is little doubt that they are very good at doing so. The relevance of the informal curriculum to their own lives is a key factor here. Children are interested in what they see around them and are good at exploring their environment on their own terms; through watching, listening, playing, talking and thinking.

In school, children are assumed to be learning only when they are 'on task' and progressing through prescribed steps within carefully planned lessons. For children learning informally there is no pre-determined approach. Children observe and listen, they ask questions, talk and discuss matters of importance with parents and with each other. As we have seen, they may channel very purposeful energy into finding out for themselves things they find interesting or consider to be important. They sustain research efforts by pursuing longer-term hobbies based on crafts or sport or other interests. They play; working through ideas, setting up scenarios, creating and imitating. The learning taking place through these activities is often barely discernible; even the purposeful pursuance of a hobby is undertaken for pleasure rather than with the intention of becoming an expert. Yet within these activities a number of cognitive strategies are employed, demonstrating that intellectual reasoning and hypothesis testing could be developed without recourse to knowledge of an academic nature. Topics such as the rules of football and the intricacies of step family relationships provide rich opportunities for the practising and honing of intellectual skills. Finally practice itself, whether through choice or through the dictates of everyday life, allow children to consolidate new skills and ideas.

Children's individual reactions to the cultural curriculum around them dictate both the pace and structure of their learning. How much they want or are able to take in from a given situation or activity at a given time may be decided by a complex of interest, mood and previous understanding. Some reactions, such as boredom, lack of concentration, inability to apply what they may have previously appeared to understand or simply doing nothing would be considered, in the classroom, to be negative and inhibiting to learning. In informal learning however, these reactions may actually be part of a self-regulatory learning system in which learners themselves subconsciously dictate if and when they are ready to take their learning further. Of course with informal learning these reactions are not likely to last for long because children simply move on to something else that has engaged their interest.

The naturalness and efficacy of this type of learning engagement is such that there is very often the feeling that children are simply learning by osmosis; absorbing the information around them in an almost effortless fashion. And indeed, much may be being taken in implicitly with barely any learner awareness of the acquisition of new knowledge. The metaphor of the sponge was one which frequently came to mind as parents described the feel of such learning.

> She just knows things that you wouldn't imagine she could know ... watching them they are like little sponges. And taking what they want, not what they have been told to take. ... I have been amazed that I have just stepped back and she's just developing. Completely and utterly on her own it feels like. ... Although I am there she is doing it for herself, she is picking up things. (24)

> They are so sponge-like and receptive to everything that maybe you are not hearing because you are not into that but they are hearing it, or seeing it or they are talking about it. (16)

Third, parents or carers play an important role in children's informal learning although what they do is not materially different to the ways in which most parents of children in school interact with them out of school hours. It is just good parenting. It includes providing a stable home background, intellectual stimulation, parent–child discussion, encouragement and general support of children's activities. Parents share their own knowledge either deliberately or implicitly, act as role models through their own engagement with the informal curriculum and facilitate access to knowledge they do not have, often sharing in the learning themselves. Most of this interaction occurs quite naturally as a consequence of shared lives rather than deliberate pedagogy and is not pre-planned or structured. Underlying it all is a faith both in their children and in the form of education which they are undertaking. Parents frequently expressed the conviction that not only were their children capable people able to learn whatever they needed in order to take up a useful and personally fulfilling place in society but also that child-led learning would ensure that this happened. As one parent neatly summed up the whole philosophy:

> I've never worried about whether they are going to be alright … I did believe that if they were happy, actually doing what they wanted to do, everything else would work itself out. And I actually believe that more now. (6)

The example of literacy, the school learning of which can cause a great deal of stress for children, teachers and parents, exemplifies the ways in which informal learning takes place as a natural part of everyday life. Children who learn to read informally do not do so as a self-contained activity, based on synthetic phonics, graded readers and suchlike. Instead their 'readers' are street and shop names, road and garage signs, cereal packets, brand names, computer prompts, and so on; written language that has real meaning for them, initiated by themselves or pointed out by their parents. They learn to read as they learn the relevance of reading in daily life; they learn what they want to read, when they want to read it. Similarly they build up literacy experience by writing birthday cards, notes, lists, labels and their own literary props when playing. Parents contribute by reading stories, joining in with children's own efforts to read and, through the course of their everyday lives, acting as role models who demonstrate the central part that literacy plays in almost every aspect of modern life.

Informal learning and the development of thinking capacity

Whilst children may learn, and may learn more than adequately in the ways we have described, critics are still likely to point to the risk that children will pick up their information peppered with misunderstandings or downright inaccuracies.

Parents may unwittingly pass on their own misconceptions and information from different sources may be contradictory or incomplete. Yet the lack of information quality control does not appear, as one might expect, to lead to muddled, confused children with a patchy understanding of what schools set out to teach. Instead, the apparent disadvantage of informal learning; that it is not structured, sequenced and ordered with the learner in mind, may well be one of the strengths.

First of all, having information deliberately broken up by other people is only helpful if the ways in which this is done make overall sense to the learner. More important than having your information broken down and sequenced may be the place and the way in which you come across it. A real-life, holistic setting from which it can be linked to other ideas and information may be what allows the learner to order information in the way which is most helpful to them.

A second consideration is that children do not simply take in information. They take it in, maybe partially, think about, put it together with other bits of information, pull it apart again or simply hang on to it for later corroboration. Many of the activities or processes we have mentioned; observation, conversation, play, intellectual search show this kind of thing going on and demonstrate that 'thinking skills' are part and parcel of engaging with the informal curriculum. Researching, following through lines of argument, hypothesis building, problem solving, comparing information, experimenting were all naturally occurring aspects of children's day-to-day and self-selected activities. They did not need to be separately introduced or linked to any specific subject matter. The cognitive strategies employed, apparently spontaneously, by children as they sought to investigate a range of topics, demonstrate that reasoning and hypothesis testing can be developed without presentation in an academic context. We saw this in relation to working out the rules of football and step family relationships (Chapters 5 and 7).

A third factor we would suggest is that the study of informal home education begins to reveal how many routes there are to the same basic achievements. Looking at the different ways in which children acquire the primary school skills of literacy and numeracy makes this abundantly clear. As one parent pointed out, if you get interested in a topic, no matter what, reading is going to come into it somewhere. So, in all probability, will some aspects of basic maths, science or social and personal development; even if these are not labelled as such. Child-led learning ensures that children are reaching these bodies of knowledge through avenues that hold an intrinsic appeal to them. Whilst debates over the efficacy of competing reading pedagogies rage on, informal learning suggests that what is of paramount importance in mastering this skill, is that children read or are helped to read what they want to read, rather than that they receive a specific type of instruction.

Fourthly, the question of motivation, so important for success in school, barely seems to arise in informal learning. Children learn because that is what they do rather than because they are in some additional way motivated to do so. Pre-school children are intrinsically motivated to explore, to play, to be with their parents and join in with other adults and children. Meeting these desires is sufficient to ensure learning for them. Our study suggests that this continues to be the case for children who carry on learning informally at home.

The overwhelming message from this study has to be the ease, naturalness and immense intellectual potential of informal learning. Children who are educated informally learn, not as a separate activity as children do in school, but as an integral part of everything they do as they engage with the world around them. We hope we have made a start in unravelling the complexity of the learning processes involved.

Appendix 1

The families

(NB. Children were often present for some of the time and contributed)

Interview participant(s)	Children educated at home and ages
1. Father	M 16; M 14
2. Mother	M 24; M 22; M 16; M 11; M 9
3. Mother	M 15; F 13; M 11; M 10; M 8
4. Both parents	F 12; F 10
5. Mother	M 14; M 11; M 9
6. Both parents	F 13; F 11; M 7
7. Mother	M 24; M 21; F 11
8. Mother	F 13; M 11
9. Mother	M 12; M 10; F 7; M 2
10. Mother	M 14; F 12
11. Mother	F 17; F 14; F 12; M 10; M 8
12. Mother	M 18; M 15; M 13; F 10
13. Mother	M 24; F 21; F 18; F 16; M 10
14. Mother	F 12; F 10; M 7
15. Both parents	F 11; M 9
16. Mother	F 20; M 18; M 14; F 6
17. Both parents	F 5; M 3; F 18 months
18. Mother	M 12; M 8
19. Father	M 10; M 8; M 6
20. Mother	M 16; F 14; F 10
21. Both (separately)	F 14; M 12

22. Mother   M 9 months
                              Herself home educated
23. Mother   M 9; F 8 months
24. Mother   F 8
25. Mother   F 6; F 4; M 18 months
26. Mother   F 19; F 17; M 14

Appendix 2

Facsimile

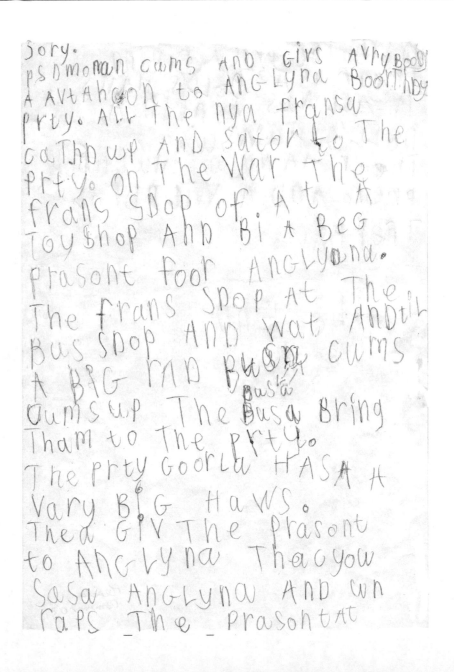

inSid The prity riping.
Thear is A Doll's HAWS
IV ALL Was Wontid A
DoLL's HaWsa.
Their HAWa a wwhhtot
prtyo AND A Wanbtot
TheP BAc.

The END

Meade
Rommer 03

References

Arnott, A., Fell, R. and Benson, R. (2001) *Stories of Learning and Change – more than can be said: The practical implications of a study of northern Australian pastoralists' learning process.* Charles Darwin University, Australia.

Bandura, A. (1977) *Social Learning Theory.* Englewood Cliffs, New Jersey, Prentice Hall.

Beard, R. (2000) *Developing Writing 3–13.* London, Hodder Arnold.

Beckett, D. & Hager, P. (2002) *Life, Work and Learning: Practice in Postmodernity.* London, Routledge.

Bendell, J. (1987) *School's Out.* London, Ashgrove Publishing.

Bennett, N., Desforges, C., Cockburn, A. & Wilkinson, B. (1984) *The Quality of Pupil Learning Experiences.* London, Lawrence Erlbaum Associates.

Bennett, N., Wood, L. & Rogers, S. (1996) *Teaching Through Play: Teachers' Theories and Classroom Practice.* Buckingham, Open University Press.

Bissex, G. L. (1980) *Gnys at Wrk – A Child Learns to Write and Read.* Cambridge, Massachusetts, Harvard University Press.

Blyth, A. (1988) *Informal Primary Education Today.* Brighton, Falmer Press.

Bremner, J. G. (1994) *Infancy.* Oxford, Blackwell.

Bruce, T. (1994) Play, the universe and everything. In: J. R. Moyles (ed.) *The Excellence of Play.* Philadelphia, Open University Press.

— (2004) *Developing Learning in Early Childhood.* London, Paul Chapman.

Carraher, T. N., Carraher, D. W. & Schliemann, A. D. (1985) Mathematics in the streets and in the schools, *British Journal of Developmental Psychology,* 3, 21–9.

Carraher, D. W. & Schliemann, A. D. (2000) Reasoning in mathematics education: realism versus meaningfulness. In: D. H. Jonassen & S. M. Land (eds) *Theoretical Foundations of Learning Environments.* New Jersey, Lawrence Earlbaum Associates.

Cohen, D. & McKeith, S. A. (1991) *The Development of the Imagination: The Private Worlds of Childhood.* London, Routledge.

Cole, M. (1998) Culture in development. In: M. Woodhead, D. Faulkener & K. Littleton (eds) *Cultural Worlds of Early Childhood.* London, Routledge.

Cullen, J., Batterbury, S., Foresti, M., Lyons, C. & Stern, E. (2000) *Informal Learning and Widening Participation.* Research Report No. 191. Nottingham, DfEE.

Desforges, C. & Abouchaar, A. (2003) *The Impact of Parental Involvement, Parental Support and Family Education on Pupil Achievement and Adjustment: A Literature Review.* London, Department for Education and Skills, Research Report No. 433.

Donaldson, M. (1978) *Children's Minds*. London, Fontana.

Douglas, J. W. B. (1967) *The Home and the School: a Study of Ability and Attainment in the Primary School*. London, Panther.

Dowty, T. (2000) *Free Range Education: How Home Education Works*. Stroud, Hawthorn Press.

Egan, K. (2005) *An Imaginative Approach to Teaching*. San Francisco, Jossey-Bass.

Entwistle, H. (1970) *Child Centred Learning*. London, Methuen.

Eraut, M. (2000) Non-formal learning, implicit learning and tacit knowledge in professional work. In: F. Coffield (ed.) *The Necessity of Informal Learning*. Bristol, The Policy Press.

Fischer, S. R. (2003) *A History of Reading*. London, Reaktion Books Ltd.

Galton, M., Simon, P. & Croll, P. (1980) *Inside the Primary Classroom*. London, Routledge and Kegan Paul.

Garrick, J. (1998) *Informal Learning in the Workplace: Unmasking Human Resource Development*. London, Routledge.

Gaskins, S. (1999) Children's daily lives in a Mayan village: A case study of culturally constructed roles and activities. In: A. Goncu (ed.) *Children's Engagement in the World – Sociocultural Perspectives*. Cambridge, Cambridge University Press.

Gauvain, M. (2001) *The Social Context of Cognitive Development*. New York, Guilford Press.

Gear, J., McIntosh, A. & Squires, G. (1994) *Informal Learning in the Professions*. Department of Adult Education, University of Hull.

Gorard, S., Fevre, R., Rees, G., Furlong, J. & Renold, E. (1998) Home and away: the decline of informal learning in South Wales 1900 - 1997. Working Paper 13, School of Education , University of Cardiff.

Griffith, M. (1998) *The Unschooling Handbook – How to Use the Whole World As Your Child's Classroom*. USA, Prima Publishing.

Guberman, S. R. (1999) Supportive environments for cognitive development: Illustrations from children's mathematical activities outside school. In: A. Goncu (ed.) *Children's Engagement in the World – Sociocultural Perspectives*. Cambridge, Cambridge University Press.

Hall, N. (1994) Play, Literacy and the role of the teacher. In: J. R. Moyles (ed.) *The Excellence of Play*. Philadelphia, Open University Press.

Heyns, B. (1978) *Summer Learning and the Effects of Schooling*. New York, Academic Press.

Hoogsteder, M., Maier, R. & Elbers, E. (1998) Adult-child interaction, joint problem solving and the structure of cooperation. In: M. Woodhead, D. Faulkener, & K. Littleton (eds) *Cultural Worlds of Early Childhood*. London, Routledge.

Ireson, J. & Blay, J. (1999) Constructing activity: participation by adults and children. *Learning and Instruction* 9, 19–36.

Jahoda, G. & Lewis, I. M. (1988) *Acquiring Culture: Cross Cultural Studies in Child Development*. London, Croom Helm.

Lave, J. & Wenger, E. (1991) *Situated Learning: Legitimate Peripheral Participation*. Cambridge, Cambridge University Press.

Lines, P. M. (2001) Homeschooling, Eric Digest 151.

Long, S. (1998) The significance of playmates in the acquisition of a second language. In: G Walford & A Massey (eds) *Studies in Educational Ethnography. Vol I: Children Learning in Context*. London, Jai Press Inc.

McMillan, G. & Leslie, M. (1998) *The Early Intervention Handbook: Intervention in Literacy*. Education Department, City of Edinburgh Council.

Medrich, E. A., Roizen, J., Rubin, V. & Buckley, S. (1982) *The Serious Business of Growing Up: A Study of Children's Lives Out of School*. Berkeley, University of California Press.

Meighan, R. (1995) Home-based education effectiveness research and some of its implications.

Educational Review, 47, 275–87.

Mercer, N. (1995) *The Guided Construction of Knowledge: Talk Amongst Teachers and Learners*. Clevedon/New York, Multilingual Matters Ltd.

Nicolaisen, I. (1988) Concepts and learning among the Punan Bah of Sarawak. In: G. Jahoda and I. M. Lewis (eds) *Acquiring Culture: Cross Cultural Studies in Child Development*. London, Croom Helm.

OFSTED (Office for Standards in Education) (1993) *First Class: The Standards and Quality of Education in Reception Classes*. London, HMSO

Opie, P. & Opie, I. (1959) *The Lore and Language of School Children*. Oxford, Clarendon Press.

Paradise, R. (1998) What's different about learning in schools as compared to family and community settings? *Human Development*, 41, 270–8.

Plowden Report (1967) *Children and their Primary Schools*. A Report for the Central Advisory Council of Education. London, HMSO.

QCA (Qualifications and Curriculum Authority) (2000) *Curriculum Guidance for the Foundation Stage*. London, Qualifications and Curriculum Authority.

Rogoff, B. (1990) *Apprenticeship in Thinking*. New York, Oxford University Press.

Rogoff, B., Paradise, R., Mejía Arauz, R., Correa-Chávez, M. & Angelillo, C. (2003) Firsthand learning through intent participation *Annual Review of Psychology*, 54, 175–203.

Rothermel, P. (2002) Home Education: Rationales, Practices and Outcomes. Unpublished PhD Thesis, University of Durham.

Saxe, G. B. (1991) *Culture and Cognitive Development: Studies in Mathematical Understanding*. Hillsdale, New Jersey, Lawrence Earlbaum Associates Inc.

Schaffer, H. R. (1996) *Social Development*. Malden, Blackwell Publishers Ltd.

Schieffelin, B. & Ochs, E. (1998) A cultural perspective on the transition from prelinguistic to linguistic communication. In: M. Woodhead, D. Faulkener & K. Littleton (eds) *Cultural Worlds of Early Childhood*. London, Routledge.

Smith, E. A. (1994) *Educating the Under-Five's*. London, Cassell.

Smith, F. (1988) *Joining the Literacy Club: Further Essays into Education*. London, Heinemann.

Smith, P. K., Cowie, H. & Bladoг, M. (2003) *Understanding Children's Development*. Oxford, Blackwell.

Smithers, R. (2004) Teaching in 1960s crackers, says inspector. *The Guardian* 6 October.

Stainthorp, R. & Hughes, D. (1999) *Learning From Children Who Read at an Early Age*. London, Routledge.

Super, C. M. & Harkness, S. (1982) The infant's niche in rural Kenya and metropolitan America. In: L. Adler (ed.) *Issues in Cross Cultural Research*. New York, Academic Press.

— (1986) The developmental niche: A conceptualization at the interface of child and culture. *International Journal of Behavioural Development*, 9, 545–70.

— (1998) The development of affect in infancy and early childhood. In: M. Woodhead, D. Faulkener & K. Littleton (eds) *Cultural Worlds of Early Childhood*. London, Routledge.

Thomas, A. (1992) Individualised teaching. *Oxford Review of Education*, 18, 59–74.

— (1994) Conversational learning. *Oxford Review of Education*, 20, 131–42.

— (1998) *Educating Children at Home*. London, Continuum International Publishing Group.

— (2005) Informal learning. In: R. Hancock & J. Collins (eds) *Primary Teaching Assistants: Learners and Learning*. London, Open University Press.

Tizard, B. & Hughes, M. (1984) *Young Children Learning at Home and in School*. London, Fontana.

Trevarthen, C. (1995) The child's need to learn a culture. In: M. Woodhead, D. Faulkner & K. Littleton (eds) *Cultural Worlds of Early Childhood*. London, Routledge.

Tudge, J., Hogan, D., Lee, S. Tammeveski, P., Meltsas, M., Snezhkova, I. & Putnam, S. (1999) Cultural heterogeneity: parental values and beliefs and their pre schoolers activities in the United States, South Korea, Russia and Estonia. In: A. Goncu (ed.) *Children's Engagement in the World – Sociocultural Perspectives*. Cambridge, Cambridge University Press.

Watson, J. D. (1968) *The Double Helix*. London, Penguin Books.

Weinberger, J. (1996) *Literacy Goes to School*. London, Paul Chapman.

Wood, D. (1998) *How Children Think and Learn*. Oxford, Blackwell Publishing.

Wood, D. J., Wood, H. A. & Middleton, D. J. (1978) An experimental evaluation of four face-to-face teaching strategies. *International Journal of Behavioural Development*, 1, 131–47.

Index